Agents of Change in Bullet Tree Falls

How a Village in Belize Responded to Influences of Globalization

Andrew J. Gordon

*Anthropology Program,
Department of Comparative Cultural Studies,
University of Houston*

CENGAGE
Learning·

Australia • Brazil • Mexico • Singapore • United Kingdom • United States

Agents of Change in Bullet Tree Falls: How a Village in Belize Responded to Influences of Globalization

Andrew J. Gordon

Product Director: Marta Lee-Perriard

Product Manager: Elizabeth A. Beiting-Lipps

Content Developer: Trudy Brown

Product Assistant: Chelsea Meredith

Marketing Manager: Kara Kindstrom

Art and Cover Direction, Production Management, and Composition: MPS Limited

Manufacturing Planner: Judy Inouye

Photo and Text Researcher: Lumina Datamatics

Cover Image: © Andrew Gordon

Library of Congress Control Number: 2015951429

ISBN: 978-1-133-60449-5

Cengage Learning
20 Channel Center Street
Boston, MA 02210
USA

Cengage Learning is a leading provider of customized learning solutions with employees residing in nearly 40 different countries and sales in more than 125 countries around the world. Find your local representative at **www.cengage.com**.

Cengage Learning products are represented in Canada by Nelson Education, Ltd.

To learn more about Cengage Learning Solutions, visit **www.cengage.com**.

Purchase any of our products at your local college store or at our preferred online store **www.cengagebrain.com**.

Printed in the United States of America
Print Number: 01   Print Year: 2015

With thoughts of my family—past, present, and future.

Contents

List of Figures

Preface

My strategy in fieldwork was to engage with diverse segments of the local community. On a particular day I might spend several hours in one of the local Pentecostal churches listening to warnings about God's vengeance on Judgment Day and how many sinners would be slain, juxtaposed against the promise of everlasting life for those who accepted Jesus as their savior. It was not unusual for me during another part of the same day to spend time mingling with other friends adorned by dreadlocks, as they swilled their rum and smoked their *spliffs* (marijuana cigarettes). I was constantly going back and forth between segments of the community whose lifestyles and philosophy of life were at odds with one another. As an anthropologist interested in cultural diversity, I sought to participate in all aspects of community life while still abiding by the country's laws.

Villagers knew all about the wide range of my friendships, often involving individuals or groups with whom they disagreed and disapproved. Despite this potential drawback, they were patient and accepting of me; they understood that my goal was to understand all expressions of village life. As in my previous episodes of ethnographic fieldwork, I reaffirmed how it is possible for strangers to find acceptance in unfamiliar places under unlikely circumstances. Students in my ethnographic field school learned this lesson as well, as they found much to be gained by being unhurried, respectful, and willing listeners to their Belizean hosts whom they allowed to become their teachers.

I started out with the limited objective of documenting the efforts of an American archeologist who intended to remake the village of Bullet Tree Falls into a destination for cultural heritage tourism. Her project sought to exhibit Maya cultural heritage, including its inherent genius for conservation, traditional crafts, and the clever use of the rainforest for producing food, medicines, hunting equipment, and building supplies. I approached my task as an applied anthropologist, taking into account the positive and negative aspects of the archeologist's plans and social interactions. From this initial investigation, I began to realize how much a remote village could be transformed by a relatively powerful individual bringing ideas and designs from another country. Then I began to notice and investigate other transformations linked to the efforts of outsiders who brought various global influences to this same locality, always maintaining my awareness that the individual is often a harbinger of change.

I was at the right time and place to observe a rush of global influences into the village. Independence had come to Belize in 1981, opening the country to the penetration of outside organizations and agents of change who stepped in to show Belizeans who they might be, what they might become. After investigating the archaeology project and its attempt to revive Maya culture, I turned my attention to post-colonial cooperative movements, which in large measure resulted from the work of the "Father of the Country" Prime Minister George Price, who expropriated the land of British colonists and turned it over to Belizeans. In pushing for the establishment of cooperatives, Price was guided by the egalitarian ethic of Catholic social justice, spread widely in Belize by trainers in cooperative development who came from a Jesuit institute in Nova Scotia. At this stage in my research I became aware of the work of other Canadians who were inspired by a capitalist business ethic to reshape the cooperative movement. Their influence, not surprisingly, undermined the success of cooperatives that strove to be egalitarian. My next set of encounters was with a charismatic figure from outside the community and his newly acquired followers espousing the Jamaican creed of Rastafarianism, including its dedication to natural foods, a non-material lifestyle, African Christianity, and plenty of *ganja*. Lastly, I became interested in tracking the religious conversion efforts of American Evangelical missionaries whose success had eroded local beliefs and rituals associated with the Catholic religion customarily practiced in Mesoamerica.

I had time on my side. My fieldwork extended over a four-year period, from 2009 through 2012, altogether encompassing eighteen months of active investigation. My engagement and personal commitments brought a different perspective on globalization than I had found in the post-1995 literature, which included 3000 books having the word "globalization" in the title, out of which about 100 were published by anthropologists. My immersion in the community of Bullet Tree Falls revealed how globalization happens concretely in person-to-person interactions, with transmissions often proceeding one person at a time. I identified different approaches to initiating change as a result of spending time both with the agents of change and with the villagers in their homes, churches, and bars. To get the full story, I went back to the sources of change, to the cultural settings and organizations of the change agents. I travelled far and wide to visit the Evangelical missionaries from Oklahoma and Miami, and to the Canadian brokers of economic change, including the Jesuits in Nova Scotia and the purveyors of the business model of cooperatives in Ontario, Canada. I visited George Price in Belize City to learn about the influence of the papal encyclicals on his politics, his pre-colonial independence movement, and his political party. I searched out and interviewed the leader of the Rastafarian movement in Bullet Tree Falls who lived on a small offshore island. Finally, I had the opportunity to check in, again and again, on village residents to record their life histories and how they had been exposed to global influences that had affected their personal lives.

Among other insights gained in the course of my investigations, I learned two basic lessons of globalization—that acceptance and rejection of new cultural forms lead to selectivity in the process of transfer from one person to another and one place to another, and that new cultural forms may emerge from conflict between the admonishments of change agents and historical ways of thinking and acting in the local setting

Throughout this book I offer the reader a personalized view of my research findings by keeping myself in the narrative and recording my reactions to what I saw and heard. I invite you, the reader, to join me to reflect upon the inside stories of globalization as I heard them from village residents, from other Belizeans, and from the architects of change around the world. Consider yourself my partner in the excitement of discovery linked to the study and analysis of change.

ACKNOWLEDGMENTS

The assistance from colleagues at the University of Houston, Program in Anthropology, Department of Comparative Cultural Studies, has been diverse and continuing, and I thank you all for your collegiality. As well, I owe a continuing debt to my professors at the University of Wisconsin—Madison. Students were an extraordinary support in this project, and I should like to name Irene Ketonen, Carminia Martinez, Alfonso Lopez, Garan Lyles, Kimberlee Schluter, and Ricky Alba. In the latter stages of my work I was very much helped by my wife Ana Maria and by Dan Gordon. Always we owe a great debt to those in the field who gave their time and friendship. Everyone in Bullet Tree Falls proved to be welcoming and helpful. They seemed to always have had the time to help me arrive at a better understanding of the world in which they lived. There are five from Belize I would like to mention, who gave so much; and, sadly, I was faced with their demise while in Belize. Heroes, all of them: Elias Awe, Heriberto Cocom, Gustavo Espat, Eduardo Espat, and the Honourable George Cadle Price. They all have contributed so much to life in Belize, and I thank them for sharing their wealth of information. Additionally, I appreciate the continuing assistance of the University of Houston small grants program for aid in research and the program of Faculty Development Leave. Above all, I owe an enormous debt to my editor John Young, who withheld nothing, gave generously, and provided a model of how to think through and present evidence from the field. Additionally, I should like to express my appreciation to the staff at Cengage, especially the diligence and patience of Jitendra Kumar in overseeing the editorial process and the able support from Trudy Brown in overall matters of production.

About the Author

Andrew J. Gordon is Associate Professor in the Anthropology program in the Department of Comparative Cultural Studies, University of Houston. He has a Ph.D. in Anthropology from the University of Wisconsin and a Master's Degree from the Harvard School of Public Health. His focus is on the application of anthropology and has concentrated on alcohol and drug use, economic development, primary care, and vector-borne diseases. He has taught in Schools of Public Health in Columbia University's School of Public Health, the John Jay College of Criminal Justice, the University of South Carolina, and currently, the University of Houston. He has taught abroad, as a Fulbright Fellow both in the Dominican Republic and in Conakry, Guinea. Gordon has worked as a consultant for the Pan American Health Organization, the Centers for Disease Control, the United States Agency for International Development, the World Bank, the World Health Organization as well as local agencies, both governmental and private.

Currently, he continues work with globalization and he is exploring a neglected focus on political culture. In his work, past and present, Gordon tends to seek a fruitful blend of varied anthropological theories along with the approaches of applied work. He has an anthropologist wife, Ana Maria, from Argentina and two children, Rebecca, an astrologer, and Dan, an actor/producer.

About this Case Study

In this book you will discover how an immigrant village in the rainforest of Belize experienced changes of major proportions brought by four disparate influences from the outside world: cultural heritage tourism, Rastafarianism, the cooperative movement, and Evangelical missionaries. Finding himself easily accepted into an open and welcoming community, the author provides revealing life stories of outside agents of change and community members who sometimes embrace and sometimes resist intentional efforts to transform their lives. Readers will be intrigued by the strategies and mechanisms of intervention designed to alter not only essential livelihoods, but also self-perceptions, symbolic allegiances, and patterns of social interaction. Comparison of the four cases reveals features typical of the workings, as opposed to the obvious trappings, of globalization, and shows why some attempts at bringing about change occur smoothly while others meet with difficulties and still others spin off in unanticipated directions. The author examines a particularly unlikely and fascinating scenario as it unfolded—romance tourism involving Rastafarian men and foreign women. Although it may seem counterintuitive, readers will learn how the intimate and effective conversion strategies of Rastafarians and Evangelicals might inform bureaucratic planners and managers—those we might otherwise consider to be the experts on change. Accounts of critical historical events and competing cultural frameworks that shaped the setting for change, both in and outside of Belize, support the author's firsthand description and analysis of global influences affecting a small community.

John A. Young
Series Editor, Contemporary Social Issues

1/Contemplating a Study of Change

On a Saturday morning in May of 1990, it was my time to sleep in. I was in Benque Viejo del Carmen, a town on the western side of Belize, near the border with Guatemala (Figure 1.1). In the previous two weeks, I had visited towns all over Belize. Located between Mexico and Guatemala, Belize encompasses just 8,666 square miles, and at that time its population was only 189,000. I was employed as a U.S. Government consultant, sent to work with the Belizean government on prevention of malaria and dengue fever,[1] both diseases spread by mosquitoes. As an applied anthropologist my main role was to develop community programs to eliminate mosquito-breeding sites.

I was glad for the break from my busy travel and work routine. Later that morning, I left my hotel to wander around and get a quick impression of the town. Much of Benque looked as if it were stuck in a previous time. Its streets were narrow, just wide enough to travel by horse, lined with houses of stone, typical of the rural towns in colonial-era Guatemala, the country of origin of many of Benque's residents, contrasting with other parts of Belize where streets tend to be wide and lined by wooden houses. Gazing around, I saw no one in the streets. Townspeople were wiser than I in avoiding the midday sun. Their socializing went on at night when people moved around leisurely, calmly chatting or glancing up to second-floor porches to greet onlookers sitting in their rocking chairs. What I did not know was that this tranquil scene was about to change in an important way, and that my walk was the beginning of a long-term study of globalization and change in Belize.

I ducked into Alma's Bar nestled in the first floor of an old building, taking a seat at one of the five wooden tables scattered about the place. Years of entering out-of-the-way places in Africa and Latin America had taught me to sit alone, to observe what was going on but not to stare, and to speak little unless approached. Men seated at two of the other tables took little notice of my presence. To them outsiders seemed commonplace: Peace Corps volunteers, American missionaries, and development workers. The men's faces were somber, their bodies thick and solid from the effects of hard work. Even though they were seated, I could tell they were short, perhaps around 5′4″ in height. They had black hair, tawny skin, and the broad and high cheekbones characteristic of Maya ancestry. They spoke in low tones as they worked their way through several bottles of beer.

Two more men entered, strode to the center of the room, and took the canvas cover off a ten-foot-long marimba, a type of wooden xylophone especially popular among the Maya in Guatemala during the nineteenth century. The instrument was

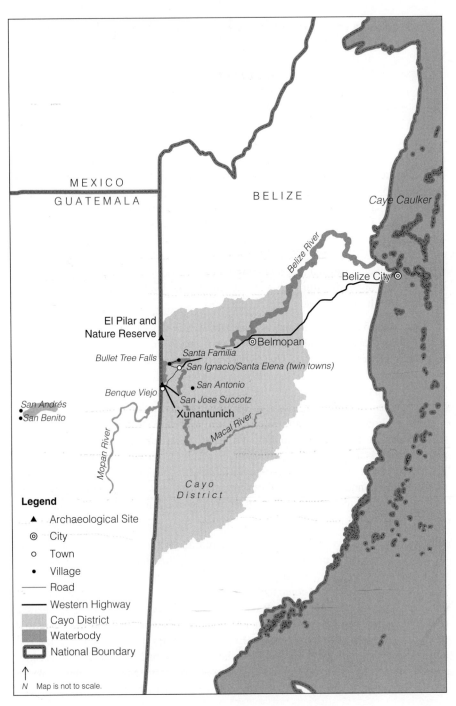

Figure 1.1 Belize.

long enough to accommodate up to three musicians standing shoulder to shoulder from one end to the other, each with three mallets in hand—eighteen mallets in all. A third man entered and approached the instrument. His growth appeared to have been stunted, perhaps by accident or illness. His demeanor seemed sad and discouraged, yet he immediately hopped onto a chair to gain the necessary height above the instrument and took his place behind the treble end of the keyboard. The lines etched in his face relaxed, and he smiled as light, melodic tones streamed forth from the three musicians.

The bar scene matched the town, with its easygoing, intimate, colonial-type atmosphere. People seemed comfortable with one another, with their routines of socializing, and with the marimba.

INDICATIONS OF CHANGE

I made my next visit to Belize in March 2003—13 years later. My purpose was to find a site suitable to host a summer field school for anthropology students from the University of Houston, where I had joined the teaching faculty. Belize was politically pro-American, safe, and not far from Texas, thus making airfare less expensive. Benque, a quiet community with an interesting Maya heritage, had immediately come to mind as a possible place for the field school. I checked into the same hotel where I had stayed 13 years earlier. At the first opportunity I searched for marimba music, assuming that it might raise curiosity among my students about Maya culture. I hoped they might conduct research projects on the cultural aspects of the music, the roles of men who make music, and the roles of women who listen; other research projects might focus on peoples' historical memories of Guatemala, and the significance of their current national identity as Belizeans. On this occasion, however, I found no marimba in Alma's Bar, which no longer hosted this type of Maya-Guatemala scene. I asked around, "Where else could I hear marimba music?" "Go to the bar called 'Los Angeles,'" people said, describing a family bar where the owners, the Castellanos brothers, had become famous not only for playing marimba music, but also for manufacturing their own instruments. Disappointment greeted me when I arrived at the Los Angeles Bar. I saw only three marimbas, all broken and appearing to be long out of use. It was apparent that marimba playing was no longer a part of public life, and no longer available for visitors as a ready exposure to Maya culture.

Other disappointments followed; most notably, people spoke too little English, preferring to speak Spanish even if they were fluent in English. In addition, I found no hotel that could adequately accommodate students, and the town had no tradition of families hosting foreign students.

I checked out another possibility seven miles away. The town of San Ignacio, along with its twin town, Santa Elena, both with a population of 14,000, twice the size of Benque, and it offered suitable facilities for student lodging. I was struck by dramatic changes that had taken place during my 13-year absence from that town. Between 1990 and 2003, San Ignacio had become a tourist gateway to the local

© Andrew Gordon

Figure 1.2 A main street in San Ignacio, 2004.

Maya world, bustling with advertisements and commerce centered on themes of Maya culture (Figure 1.2). Minibuses run by local tour companies, Mayawalk and Maya Adventure, shuttled tourists to Maya archeological sites, while restaurants offered Maya pizzas and Maya hamburgers—standard fare mixed with a token amount of *chaya*, a local green vegetable associated with the historic Maya diet. Shops and clinics touted products and services for Maya spiritual remedies. On billboards, one resort promised "The Full Mayan Experience," though it was not clear to me how a swimming pool, bar, restaurant, and modern hotel rooms resembled the Maya world.

I decided on San Ignacio as the home base for the field school. Fortunately, it turned out to be a productive site for field research, where students became intrigued with investigating the effects of tourism, including the town's newly found fame, the local rationale for belief in the superiority of the Maya diet, and the receptiveness of Belizean men to foreign women. A multitude of bars, restaurants, dance clubs, and Internet cafes kept students content during their leisure hours (Figure 1.3).

THE ATTRACTIONS OF TOURISM

Tourism only relatively recently became a staple for the Belizean economy. Before independence in 1981, the colonial economy was based on export agriculture, including sugar, bananas, citrus, and forest and marine products.

© Andrew Gordon

Figure 1.3 Students in Ethnographic Field School; author Andrew Gordon is third from the left.

From 1984 to 1990, the tourist industry became the focus of economic development in Belize, steadily rising from seventh to second place in economic output by the end of the decade. Policymakers initially promoted Belize's Gulf Coast because of its swimming beaches and opportunities for diving and fishing. By the 1990s, the policy moved away from the regional promotion of leisure activities, instead emphasizing cultural heritage tourism to attract relatively affluent visitors from around the world to marvel at magnificent archeological sites reconstructed by two generations of renowned archeologists.

In 1988, Belize became part of the European Union's five-country tourism development scheme, called "Mundo Maya," which also included Mexico, Guatemala, Honduras, and El Salvador. These countries marketed themselves as part of a Maya world boasting of a 2,000-year history and ancient cultural traditions continuing into the present. Visitors flocked to Mundo Maya, able to explore awe-inspiring archeological sites and purchase cultural commodities the present-day Maya had to offer, including crafts, cuisine, music, and herbal medicine.

Students in my field school were intrigued by the Maya world, two of them later going on to earn advanced degrees by writing theses about Maya traditions kept alive in the present day. In 2005, these two students, Carminia Martinez and Alfonso Lopez, explored the outcome of the work of Rosita Arvigo,[2] an alternative healer originally from the United States whose writings made Belize famous as a sanctuary for Maya healing. As a foreign novice, Arvigo had learned about Maya healing from her mentor, Eligio Panti, an indigenous healer who resided in San Antonio, a village eight miles from San Ignacio. Arvigo later wrote a book about

Panti, and for a period of time acquired rights to 6,000 acres provided by the Belizean government for cultivation of medicinal herbs. She also received a $100,000 grant from the United States Agency for International Development for the Terra Nova Medicinal Plant Reserve, its purpose being to organize Belizean healers as well as an association to share knowledge and disseminate Maya healing. For political reasons, the Terra Nova project was short lived. But Arvigo started a medicine trail near San Ignacio called Ix Chel exhibiting a variety of plants for medicinal use. The medicine trail was largely for visitors, a walk along a carefully manicured trail in the woods that has been cultivated and labeled with herbal plants. Medicine trails can be a half a mile long, at most, and seek to edify the outside world. The Terra Nova project, on the other hand, was for Belizean healers, not outsiders.

Arvigo's legacy is large, having opened up the science of Maya healing to the rest of the world through her writing and seminars. International visitors, fascinated by indigenous medicine and intrigued by "new age" themes and Maya architecture, started coming to San Ignacio, many of them seeking to meet personally with local Maya healers. All the healers were aware of the cachet connected with Panti and claimed him as their individual mentor.

FIRST ENCOUNTER WITH BULLET TREE FALLS

One day I accompanied Carminia and Alfonso on a short trip to Bullet Tree Falls, a village three miles west of San Ignacio with a population of 3,400, where they interviewed its two most distinguished healers, Don Beto Cocom and Don Gavriel Tsib. (*Don* is the Spanish term of honor, uttered with far more gravity than simply saying *Señor*). Upon entering the village, we could not miss the imposing presence of a cultural center called *Be Puk Te*, in Maya, meaning "On the Way to Bullet Tree." Larger than other houses, its floor plan measured 40 by 20 feet. Stepping inside the cultural center, we noticed stacks of clothing and pottery made by villagers, maps on the wall about the nearby archeology project, and small tables displaying snacks for visitors. We introduced ourselves to the manager, Doña Betty, and engaged her with questions. (*Doña* is the Spanish term of respect for a woman.) Our entire conversation was in Spanish, the language of everyday life in the village. Although Belize is an English-speaking country where children learn English in school, the most predominant language in many villages, such as Bullet Tree Falls, is Spanish.

Anabel Ford, an American archeologist, found funding for this cultural center as part of her work on the nearby Maya site of El Pilar, the administrative and theocratic center of a Maya city-state that reached its peak development more than a thousand years ago. Tourists entering the village of Bullet Tree Falls would first stop at the cultural center to buy tickets and view an informative exhibit interpreting the El Pilar site. After a visit to the site, tourists might return to the center to purchase Maya-style artisan goods and have a Maya-style snack before leaving the village.

In a calm and highly knowledgeable manner, Doña Betty informed us about the work of Anabel Ford, the archaeologist who wanted to make El Pilar an important stop on the travel itineraries of Belize-bound tourists, and promote the village as the "Gateway to El Pilar." Doña Betty added that Ford was responsible for reviving traditional Maya crafts and beginning the annual Fiesta of El Pilar, a major day-long celebration attracting visitors from all over the country. We also learned how Ford promoted organic farming and local knowledge of flora and fauna. Most important, she wanted villagers to be proud and show off their Maya heritage, another step to a successful tourism industry showing off Mundo Maya cultural heritage.

DEFINING AND EXPANDING THE FOCUS OF RESEARCH

As an anthropologist having traveled and worked on several continents, I have always been fascinated by the influence of Americans working abroad. Doña Betty's descriptions piqued my interest in Bullet Tree Falls as a venue for research into the influence of a prominent American archaeologist who had brought substantial change to the community. In my sabbatical year, 2009, I settled in Bullet Tree Falls to begin a study that I thought would be manageable because it had a clear focus on a smaller village population, mostly of Maya heritage, in an area of limited geographical scope.

The focus of my information gathering at first was on Anabel Ford, El Pilar, and the descendants of Maya settlers. Both from my own observations and from testimony of villagers employed by Ford's project, I soon became keenly aware of other global influences from Canada, Jamaica, and the United States impacting the village. Villagers told me about the cooperative movement that came from Canada in the 1980s, investing in cooperative enterprises in the village and later supporting artisan work and retail sales of Maya craft items. Early in my research, I noticed the wafting odor of marijuana, the rhythmic sounds of reggae music, and men with their hair in dreadlocks, thus becoming aware of the presence of villagers of African descent and Rastafarian affiliation. Finally, I watched adults and children walking on their way to the Evangelical Protestant churches that were overwhelming the village traditions of the Catholic Church. The villagers told stories about American Evangelical missionaries who had founded these new churches, intensifying my interest in other outside influences. As a result, I resolved to expand my study to all four interventions and their influences to fashion a broader and more comprehensive study of globalization.

DIFFERENT KINDS OF GLOBALIZATION

One day in an impromptu discussion of my research, a colleague at my university remarked that the examples of globalization I had been studying did not fit with the kinds of globalization often described in the social sciences literature. Instead of looking at one global incursion, I was intrigued by the workings of different programs of intentional change manifested in a single setting, in this case the promotion of cultural heritage tourism, the spread of the Rastafarian movement, the effort to establish cooperatives, and the life-changing commitment found among members of Evangelical churches. My focus in study of globalization was not the quite common representation of homogeneous global commerce as it crosses international borders, endlessly recreating imitations of itself: the Walmarts, McDonald's, Pizza Huts, or matters of lifestyle and taste as found in music, fashion, and public attitude. Also, my interests were more narrowly defined than those of researchers who study the far-reaching effects of the digital and media world of television, films, the radio, the Internet, and smartphones.

Instead, I followed my career interests, consistent with my work as an applied anthropologist in studying community-based ventures that are part of health care education and economic development. My concern with globalization continued my commitments to observe impacts of quite purposeful changes, often through programs, that happen to be imposed on communities, but coming from sources all over the globe.

How to manage change is a vital topic, important to a variety of constituencies such as activists, funders, program investors, and those simply with the notion and commitment that they could make the world a better place. In Bullet Tree Falls, I could examine, in one locale, how different mechanisms of change were at work in the transmission of new ideas and lifestyles. I could see how the changes moved from one person to another, across cultural divides—spanning the gap between their original source and their destination in the local village context. In a fundamental sense, initiating and experiencing change are intimate processes deeply rooted in the human propensity to engage in trade and cultural exchanges across geographical boundaries. In sum, my ethnographic study was about how people throughout the world relate to others—internationally, nationally and locally—to create a more satisfying future for Bullet Tree villagers.

THE USE OF MULTIPLE THEORIES

Because the interventions I studied were different from each other, I found it useful to adopt several distinct theoretical positions to assist in gaining a thorough understanding of each case.[3] In Chapter 2 on cultural heritage tourism, I examine Anabel Ford as a patron, drawing on theory about how patrons and clients structure their patterns of reciprocities. In Chapter 3, on Rastafarians, Reggae, and the African heritage, I rely on theory about the diffusion of persuasive messages from one culture to another in what anthropologist Arjun Appadurai calls "scapes." In Chapter 4, I focus on the idea of "imagined communities" as a way of describing the process of designing and imposing cooperatives, burdened with a set of predetermined routines, rules, and aspirations, on villagers in another part of the world. In Chapter 5, on Evangelicals, I describe the power of the narratives transmitted by missionaries to convert followers and commit them to a different kind of spirituality and new way of life. In Chapter 6, the conclusion, I generalize about processes of change from comparison of the four cases, and I offer a summary of several emergent

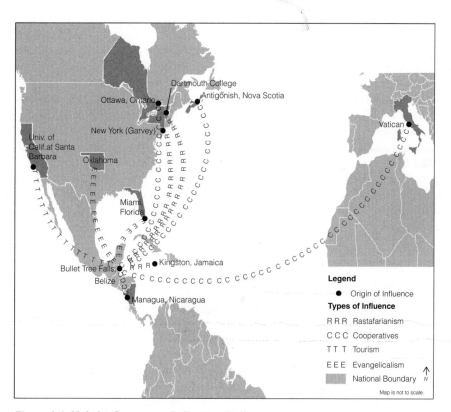

Figure 1.4 Global influences on Bullet Tree Falls.

characteristics of globalization and the ways that applied anthropologists and others can have a positive influence on programs of change (see Figure 1.4 Global Influences on Bullet Tree Falls).

COMMUNITY HISTORY, CHARACTERISTICS, AND COMPOSITION

The majority of people in Bullet Tree Falls were descendants of refugee populations that began arriving almost a century earlier. Historically, the vast majority of villagers were tied to near subsistence agriculture. They had no elite strata of leaders with civil and religious authority, a so-called "civil-religious hierarchy," common among Mesoamerican communities colonized by the Spanish, and consequently no local political elite whose self-interest might be threatened by change. Still undergoing a long process of putting down firm roots, villagers were open to new ways of life. Living in a new setting, in a recently independent and developing nation, they saw a real chance for improving their lives beyond the standards and limitations they had previously known.

Maya Origins in Mexico and Guatemala

Refugees from Mexico abandoned their homes and settled in Belize to escape the Caste War (1847–1901) in the Yucatan, which is located just to the north of Belize. (The Yucatan is Mexico's giant peninsula of 15,000 square miles that juts into the Gulf of Mexico.) In the nineteenth century, a coalition of rebellious Maya in the Yucatan tried to expel Spanish colonizers, but dissension within their ranks caused them to splinter into two separate groups at war with each other. One of these groups, the so-called Peaceful Rebels *(Sublevados Pacíficos)*, escaped this internal conflict by crossing the international border into Belize. At first, they moved from one location to another to find suitable land to farm. Each time they tried to settle down, the English-owned Belize Estates Company, which controlled large tracts of land committed to timber production, chased them away. In the early part of the twentieth century, they arrived and remained in Bullet Tree Falls.

Guatemalan refugees also migrated to Bullet Tree Falls at the same time, leaving Guatemala to escape excessive taxation, forced conscription into the army, and other government policies they considered to be oppressive. One group, mostly originating from San Benito, located two hours away by car from Bullet Tree Falls, were mixed with descendants of slave populations, previously under the domination of Spanish colonists and the Maya. In Belize, people refer to them as the "Black Spanish."

A lighter-skinned group of refugees came from the Guatemalan town of San Andrés, located about the same distance from Bullet Tree Falls as San Benito. This group originally looked as if they were Spanish, with little apparent trace of having mixed genetically with Africans or Maya. However, during the course of the twentieth century, their children, grandchildren, and great-grandchildren intermarried with others in the village, and their descendants no longer appear to be European.

Through the decades, both Mexican and Guatemalan refugees have continued to recognize their Maya heritage, calling themselves Mestizos, to reference their mix of Spanish and Indian background. I have chosen to refer to them using a more specific term, "Maya-Mestizo," as proposed by Benque writer and intellectual David Ruiz.

Creoles

Creoles, those of African heritage according to Belizean terminology, have been part of the Bullet Tree Falls population since the 1950s, when a Creole family arrived from San Ignacio. By the 1980s, they had established a culturally and economically distinct enclave, usually preferring to speak English and rarely participating in farming.

Creoles originally came to Belize in the eighteenth century as slaves brought from Africa and transported through Jamaica.[4] At first, the British only needed a few slaves organized into small teams to extract color dyes from logwoods (a species of flowering tree). During the early nineteenth century, larger teams of slaves numbering up to fifty, harvested mahogany and shipped the lumber down the rivers to the port of Belize City, to await transport to Europe.

At the beginning of the nineteenth century, two thousand slaves were living in Belize, comprising 75 percent of its population. After slavery ceased in 1838, Africans became an impoverished class of low-wage earners working for the timber industry, both in the forests and on the docks in Belize City. Some of these workers intermarried with British colonists and established their own enclave of genetically mixed people. Decades later, some of their descendants became part of an aristocratic landowning class.

During the twentieth century, the portion of the population with African ancestry became increasingly smaller. In 1946, 60 percent of the Belizean population were estimated to be African or European-Africans, shrinking in 1980 to 40 percent, and in 2010 to 21 percent, as compared to 50 percent Mestizo, 10 percent pure Maya, and 5 percent Garifuna, another culturally and historically distinct Black population originating in the Caribbean. Even though they are now in the minority, Creole preferences in music and the Creole language (a mix of English, African and Maya elements) are prominent in all parts of the country, even in Spanish-speaking villages.[5]

Recent International Settlers

International settlers, mostly from North America, constitute a fourth group who began arriving in Belize at the turn of the twenty-first century. Some resided in Bullet Tree Falls on a part-time basis while maintaining a primary residence in the United States or Canada. Others settled into year-round homes in locations pleasing to expatriate sensibilities, sometimes purchasing farmland or settling along the river that runs through the village. By 2010, about 100 settlers from North America and Europe lived in and near the village, either during vacations or on a full-time basis.

RESEARCH SETTING

During my time in Bullet Tree Falls, I interviewed members of each of the ethnic groups in the village, as well as political leaders, agency administrators, and activists in the capital city of Belmopan (population 13,931) and Belize City (population 67,964). I also called or visited in person with key individuals residing in Ottawa, Nova Scotia, Oklahoma, Vancouver and Miami who were responsible for initiating and implementing change in Belize and Bullet Tree Falls. Though I enjoyed my work outside the village, I was most comfortable pursuing my work in Bullet Tree Falls with its endless hospitality, gorgeous scenery, and tranquil atmosphere.

In contrast to my busy life in Houston, I learned to enjoy daily routines of the village without all the distracting choices of restaurants, things to buy, and places to go. It was a setting where I could dedicate myself to interviewing local residents and observing the social scene. Modern infrastructure had already come to Bullet Tree Falls—electricity in the 1980s, plumbing in the 1990s, and a paved road connecting the village to San Ignacio in the 1990s. Most houses were simple wooden structures, usually no more than a decade or two old. Since the local weather was rarely cold, people often sat outside their homes quite ready to strike up a conversation with any passersby. Despite the inevitable factionalism arising from a diverse population, residents of all kinds made clear to me that they were proud of their community, fond of surrounding farmland and forests, and that they especially cherished the river, bathing in it quite often.

2/Cultural Heritage Tourism

Tourism connected to Mundo Maya was a major impetus for change. Much of the interior of Belize became an attractive vacation destination thanks to many arche- ologists who excavated and reconstructed ancient Maya administrative and cere- monial monuments, and opened them to visitors in spectacular displays of tall pyramids, priestly residences, plazas, and cascades of stairways. Reconstructed Maya city-states appealed to visitors who wanted to see an authentic and complete version of history as it might have appeared in ancient times a thousand or more years ago.

CONSERVATION AND ARCHEOLOGY

The American archeologist Anabel Ford took a different approach, turning away from architectural reconstruction, and choosing instead to explore Maya conserva- tion practices that she believed had much to teach the contemporary world.[1] Her "mission," as she called it, was to show the relationship between Maya culture and nature in what she called the Maya "nature–culture nexus." Her work indicates that many of the ancient farming and forestry methods were indigenous forms of conservation of nature. In addition to excavating an archeological site, her plan was to establish a forest reserve that would also be relevant to the present. The reserve would demonstrate the richness of the forest that afforded opportunities, both past and present, for hunting wild game, foraging for food, gathering herbal medicine, and extracting building materials (see Figure 2.1 for distribution of heri- tage tourism sites).

Background on Ford

In 1973, Ford was well into her quest to learn about the Maya as a student at the University of California, Santa Barbara, and in 1981 she received her Ph.D. As part of her doctoral research in 1978, she studied a 18.6-mile trail between two archeological sites in Guatemala, a stretch of land later named after her as "Anabel's Trail" ("La Brecha Anabela"). She focused her inquiry on the past lives and culture of Maya commoners—those who gained their livelihood from the land as farmers— a departure from the usual exploration of sites that highlighted the activities of civil administrators, religious leaders, and merchants previously inhabiting the populous centers of Maya city-states.

The work of archeologists in Guatemala was severely limited due to civil insur- rections in the 1980s. The government's genocidal policies toward the Maya and the resulting insurgencies of people's militias made life difficult for archeologists. After leaving Guatemala, Ford moved to Belize, and in 1985, she initiated the Belize River Archeological Settlement Survey to examine rural settlement patterns similar to those she had observed in Guatemala. Her research focused on ancient farmers living in hamlets in the area near San Ignacio, in Cayo, one of six districts in the country, located on the western border of Belize, midway on a north-south axis.

The focus on the Belize River Archeological Settlement Survey became secondary in Ford's work when Belizean archeologists led to her awareness of the remains of the Maya city-state, which became known as El Pilar, situated eight miles from Bullet Tree Falls. Fascinated by this site, Ford started excavation work in 1993. At its peak, from around 600 A.D. to 1000 A.D. (the Post-Classic Period of Maya prehistory), the site held 128 acres of monumental structures of obvious political, economic, and religious grandeur.

The Promise of Cultural Revival

In the eyes of many in Bullet Tree Falls, Ford's El Pilar project brought promise and optimism about economic growth associated with a Maya cultural revival. She helped organize a community-based group called "Friends of El Pilar" (*Amigos de El Pilar*, also referred to as Amigos) to provide support and guidance to the project and to foster a local sense of ownership of the El Pilar project. With encouragement from Ford, many villagers involved in near-subsistence farming anticipated finding work as knowledgeable stewards of Maya culture, guiding visitors to explore the El Pilar site and walking with them on ancient trails. Villagers would be living examples of authentic Maya life. Many of those not employed as tour guides would be engaged in manufacturing and selling crafts or managing sideline enterprises to provide visitors with food and lodging. Villagers committed to the project hoped to earn enough money to pay for schooling for their children, electricity, water, store-bought clothes, and household amenities, such as refrigerators and televisions. They regarded the El Pilar project as their ticket to prosperity lasting into future generations.

Ford had the right idea at the right moment. Recommended policy on tourism emphasized the importance of festivals, folklore, handicrafts, history, local cuisine, and music as keys to advancing the nation's tourist industry.[2] In 2010, 17 years after Ford had started her excavations at El Pilar, I asked villagers for their observations and opinions on the early years of her work. They recalled frequently seeing a young and energetic Ford, always vibrant and lean, as she remained even in later years. They were impressed that she often brought Belizean government officials and the country's most prominent lawyers to visit her project.

SEEKING LOCAL SUPPORT

Ford designed, organized, and administered the entire El Pilar project. She embraced the limelight and took on enormous responsibilities, cobbling together a work plan, quite ingeniously, with considerable insight and energy; and to her

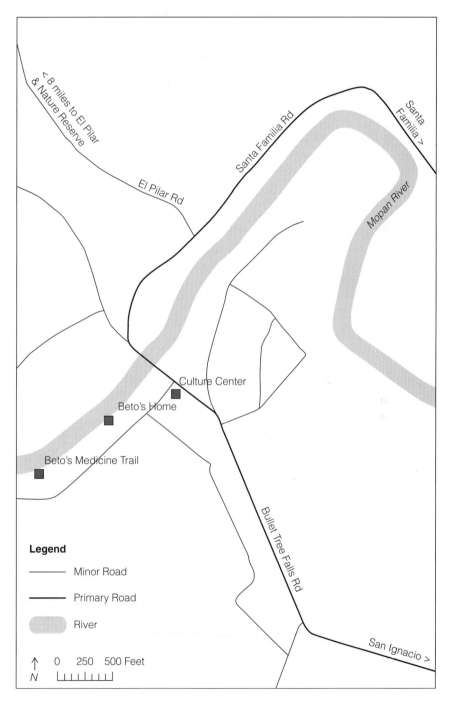

Figure 2.1 Village center-cultural heritage tourism sites.

credit, she involved villagers in much of the work. Ford's role was complex—an employer of a local workforce, benefactor of the community at large, and champion of reconstructing Maya traditions on which to build a local tourism industry. The diversity of the village population provided many constituencies from which she could potentially find support. However, the reality of securing local support was another matter.

Maya Speakers

Maya speakers, considered by villagers to be the only real Maya (Mayeros as they called themselves), would appear to have been a ready following for Ford, likely to be eager to join the project and promote the reestablishment of Maya conservation practices. However, at the beginning of my investigations in 2009, I checked around the village and found only 30 people who could speak the Maya language, all but a few of them expressing any interest in ancient Maya cultural practices. They had long ago abandoned any thoughts of a Maya revival, believing that preservation of their language was already a lost cause. A typical comment was, "That's all over now." Such skeptics typically were not open to persuasion and kept their distance from the El Pilar project.

Activists with Maya Identity

Most villagers of Maya descent who could not speak the language described themselves as Mestizos (meaning those with Maya and Spanish ancestry). In the 1980s some members of this group did gain a new appreciation for history and became attached to their Maya roots. Mostly, they had been students who had returned from abroad after having completed a university education in the United States, Cuba, Nicaragua, Jamaica, and elsewhere. Away from home, they experienced an enlightened world, where they learned the value of multiculturalism and taking pride in their indigenous ancestral heritage. Upon their return they formed an organization called The Maya Way (in Mayan, *Ix Kuxtal Masewal*) to agitate for expanded educational opportunities, identify discriminatory practices, and safeguard and revive the Maya language. Chapters of the Maya Way sprang up throughout the country, including one in Bullet Tree Falls.

The political agenda of the Maya Way contrasted with the cultural emphasis of the El Pilar project and its support group, the Amigos, though at first there appeared to be a harmony of interests as expressed by Don Epifanio, the founder of the chapter of the Maya Way in the village. With Ford's blessing he became the first president of Amigos group. His physical presence was formidable as was his influence on others who similarly identified with Maya cultural revival and surrounding politics. His appearance was reminiscent of a statue of a husky Olmec shaman, the Olmec having left their mark on the landscape in the form of statues they constructed in the Yucatan over 2,500 years ago. Don Epifanio had a large head, massive body, and thighs the girth of most men's waists. Endowed with powers of persuasion equal to his appearance, he was effective in encouraging participation in Ford's project. However, in the long run, Don Epifanio concentrated his efforts on Maya activism, civil rights, and education, having far less inclination to support Anabel Ford's interest in ancient conservation practices. One year later, he quit the Amigos groups and dedicated himself to working with other Maya activist groups in the south of Belize and in neighboring countries. At the same time, other members of the Maya Way also disengaged from the activities of the Amigos group because of other more compelling interests in their work and family and really very little desire to spend the time learning Mayan.

Evangelical Resistance

Evangelicals comprised a large segment of the Bullet Tree Falls population, numbering about 800 in 2010, many of them already having converted to the Evangelical faith before Ford began her work in 1993. Almost all were not disposed to support Ford's agenda; they expressed a harsh view of the Maya past, considering it to be the "Dark Ages" of paganism, when people worshipped false gods and knew nothing of Christ. Embracing the myths of their ancient culture was to follow the prophesy of Satan. The Evangelical Protestant way was the only way, they thought, and they resisted identification with their Maya heritage, especially its spiritual beliefs.

Job Seekers

Ford was able to attract a following of culturally inspired villagers, swayed by the opportunity to earn steady wages working for her project. Many of the 85 who signed up as members of the Amigos de El Pilar were descendants of refugees from Mexico and Guatemala. They often worked for short periods of time on the archeological excavations, and a small number took jobs in maintenance and security at the archeological site and the adjacent nature reserve. Others who were mostly women provided support services, such as preparing food and doing laundry for the archeology crew, as well as skilled artisan work, producing pottery and blouses for sale to tourists. In addition to providing wages for work, Ford intended to prepare villagers for diverse occupations in tourism, offering them special training in organic farming and artisan work. She made it possible for villagers to travel to other places in Belize and nearby Guatemala where they gained firsthand experience with tourism and organic farming—two features of the local economy that she thought would become increasingly important.

A Most Favored Follower

Don Beto Cocom, a descendent of the refugees from Mexico, was one of Ford's most favored followers. She featured him as the face of Maya heritage on the El Pilar project Website, where his photo appeared in printed promotional materials as well as in magazine publications aimed at devotees of cultural heritage tourism (see Beto relaxing at home, Figure 2.2). Don Beto told me that he felt grateful for the

© Andrew Gordon

Figure 2.2 Don Beto relaxing in his home.

recognition and Ford's attention, particularly in spreading the story about his work as a forest gardener and indigenous healer. Ford brought him international fame.

Ford also provided Don Beto with assistance from volunteer laborers to establish a medicine trail consisting of a half-mile of growing plants, most of them used for healing. Visitors walking along the trail encountered different kinds of plants, each identified by a sign bearing the plant's name in Latin and Maya, accompanied by a description of its use in healing. The medicine trail was a source of income for Don Beto, as each visitor paid BZ $15 (US $7.50), though he reduced the cost for visiting school children and groups of tourists. No stranger to marketing his services, he posted signs for tourists at all the major hotels, alerting them to the possibility of walking along the trail.

In addition to his work for Ford, Don Beto was employed by the Cornerstone Foundation, a local non-government organization (NGO) promoting social justice, public health, and the preservation of indigenous culture. His work with the Cornerstone Foundation highlighted his talents as a healer and brought many tourists to his medicine trail.

He treated patients who came to him from the Cayo region and beyond, often receiving as much as BZ $5 to BZ $10 per visit (US $2.50 to US $5) to deal with a variety of illnesses and injuries such as fevers, gastrointestinal complaints, diabetes, and cancers, and problems like dislocated muscles and bones. Many times I stopped by his house to find him sitting outside on the porch waiting for patients to come by. I observed him on one occasion treating a neighbor's child who was suffering from uncontrollable shakes during her sleep. He recited a biblical psalm accompanied by a priestly gesture of the sign of the cross, wishing the child to be cured; and because the patient was a child, he charged no fee for his services. He successfully treated me for a sprained foot that would have cost hundreds of dollars in the U.S. for medical treatment. I voluntarily paid him US $15 (BZ $30) and later made several monetary contributions to his clinic and the construction of a new consultation office outside his home. He reported having treated other international patients as well, including one American admirer who paid off a BZ $6,000 (US $3,000) bill Don Beto owed to a Mexican hospital in 2011. Despite his several occupations, Don Beto frequently appeared to be without any money, using candles to light his house, never replacing worn-out furniture, eating and dressing modestly. It seemed that his priority for his using his modest income was to help support his daughter and her three children.

Although Don Beto was overtly loyal to Ford, he kept his distance. His primary commitment was to be a healer and a spiritual leader, which meant giving less time to Maya conservation practices. He told me that he had become a healer due to his association with Don Gavriel, his brother-in-law, who introduced him to the art of Maya healing and associated spiritual rituals. Don Beto was already favorably disposed to Maya beliefs, having been close to his father who had been one of five traditional practitioners of Maya rites in the village during the 1940s and '50s. At that time, these five men were the only ones keeping alive the historic Maya rituals. After his father died, Don Beto's brother-in-law Don Gavriel took over as his mentor. Don Gavriel was hampered by a drinking problem that often left him inept with patients. As might be necessary, Don Beto filled in for him in tending to patients at Don Gavriel's residence, which served as a small hospital for Maya healing. In having this opportunity to gain hands-on experience, Don Beto became more accomplished and eventually established himself as the number-one healer in the village.

Don Beto's posture interacting with Ford was always deferential, often avoiding two-way communication about problems she might face. Though appreciative of Ford's efforts, he found it difficult to fully participate in her project and be helpful as a confidant. He did not feel that he was in a strong enough position to make comments. Gaining access, let alone giving advice, was especially difficult for Don Beto because Ford was so often caught up in a swirl of activity—countless appointments, phone and email messages, proposals to write, and community events to plan.

A SPARSELY ATTENDED RITUAL

When I first visited the Cultural Center in Bullet Tree Falls in 2005, accompanied by Carminia and Alfonso, a lack of enthusiasm for Ford's Maya renewal was apparent. During our two-hour conversation with Doña Betty, we were the only visitors, no tourists! Several years later, in examining government statistics,

I found that only 566 visitors were recorded as having come to the El Pilar site in 2005.

Four years later in 2009, records show that the number of visitors at El Pilar had not increased. I could find slim evidence of any interest in historic Maya culture around the village, despite Ford's efforts. The lack of interest was apparent one evening when I attended a Maya ceremony in which Don Beto was officiating. The ceremonial site was on top of "The Mound," a leveled-off stretch of land at the crest of a sharply rising hill right next to the Cultural Center *in* the middle of the village. Villagers regarded this hill as historically significant because of its unnaturally steep slope, rising 30 feet above ground level, thus showing itself to be an artifact of the ancient Maya. The mound was typical of many ancient cultural sites in Belize, where one might see steep inclines overgrown with bushes grasses and trees, covering up temples, pyramids, and priestly residences abandoned long ago.

In conducting the ceremony Don Beto kept the ancestral Maya rituals alive, though it seemed primarily for his own satisfaction. At age 75, he looked like Hollywood's choice for the casting of a Maya medicine man—short, wiry, and grey-bearded, with olive skin, a large nose, and eyes fixed in a permanent squint. His appearance was dashing, as he was adorned in white slacks, a white shirt, and a white head wrap. He moved around, in a half dance, half trot, circling a 10-foot-wide bonfire, while mysteriously intoning Maya words that none of the few onlookers understood. Maya speakers from the village who could have interpreted for us were not in attendance.

Witnesses to Don Beto's performance included Juan Cano, a 35-year-old tour guide and grandson of a villager. He lived and worked in San Ignacio, but depended on Don Beto to entertain the tourists he brought to Bullet Tree Falls. Juan's friend, Alice, who also lived in San Ignacio, carried a video camera to film the performance. Maria, a woman of about 60 years of age who lived in Bullet Tree Falls, observed the proceedings with intense curiosity, consistent with her reputation as the community busybody, wanting to know what was going on everywhere and offering unsolicited comments about everything. Juan's young cousin commented that he was drawn to the occasion by the smell of incense drifting across the village. Our group of spectators, numbering five in all, included only two local villagers. "There should be more people," I thought. After all it was Sunday, a day without work, and at 6 P.M., a time at which only a small group of Catholic faithful would be at the 6:30 P.M. mass. At the end of the ceremony I passed by the Cultural Center, and noticed its three-by-four-foot sign laying on the ground, covered with dirt, an indication that it had been neglected for a long time. Remnants of the Maya world were not attracting much attention.

A MAJOR EVENT

In a system called "slash and burn" agriculture, each single family farm, or *milpa*, was controlled by a *milpero* farmer who grew corn, beans, squash, and other cultivars, for two or three seasons before the crops depleted nutrients from the soil.

© Andrew Gordon

Figure 2.3 A rancho. The milpero's *midday resting place on* milpa *lands.*

The farmer then burned unused vegetation and moved on to clear and cultivate crops on another tract. On the depleted land nutrients from the burned vegetation and new wild growth restored the soil's richness over a period of several years. When the land had been restored, the farmer could move back and begin cultivation again. This process, called slash and burn farming, continuously repeated itself in allowing fallow periods between plantings to restore the soil.

Harvests from the *milpa* fed the farmer's family and produced a surplus sold in the market. To be a *milpero* farmer was a source of honor and pride, and was part of an essential social identity of residents in Bullet Tree Falls. They have held onto their traditions of *milpa* farming, continuing to cultivate 180 *milpas*, while farmers in other villages have chosen to sell their land and become laborers travelling around the country in search of work (see Figure 2.3 for a shot of the daytime resting place commonly found on *milpas*).

This historic pattern of farming was threatened in 1994, when the U.S. Agency for International Development provided Ford with the funds necessary to map out her proposed nature reserve intended to encompass 2,000 acres adjacent to the El Pilar archeological site. During the following year she worked with the Belize Lands Department and the Department of Archeology to clear and alter a landscape already occupied by 36 *local* farmers, who eked out a living on their own family farms, or *milpas*. Although many were interested in Ford's project they were not ready to give up the land that provided their essential livelihood to promote conservation. Letters went out to the farmers telling them to vacate their farms and make way for the reserve. The government provided monetary compensation to farmers who held legitimate titles, amounting to an average of BZ $250 (US $125), which they considered a paltry sum in exchange for 50 acres. Some few, however, received considerably more money were they to have invested time and labor in planting of fruit trees and digging wells. Those without titles were considered squatters by the government and received no monetary compensation. In all cases, farmers were displeased. They believed that they had inalienable rights to the land. They were Belizeans after all, and they were engaged in working the land; it was unreasonable to kick them out.

All displaced farmers, regardless of monetary compensation, had the option of farming on available government lands in the Yalbac Hills, 20 miles away; but they considered this offer to be absurd since the one-way trip to the Yalbac took two hours by car on bad roads, not to mention that only a few farmers had access to a car. Their outrage reached the national stage on March 19, 1995, when the *Belize Times* claimed that Ford was "pressuring the farmers and succeeding in keeping them off their own lands" while they had no other way to make a living. When farmers resisted, the Belizean Defense Force showed up to remove them off the land.

Angry Villagers

I was curious to know how villagers felt about the loss of farmland. One displaced farmer who was eager to express his negative point of view guided me around the village to meet with others those who shared his critical assessment of Ford, hoping that I would be his revenge-seeking mouthpiece. I did not object to the biased sample because I was just beginning my research, and any new contacts might be helpful.

Later I made an effort to gather counterbalancing points of view. I did find that a few displaced farmers found jobs working in maintenance or as guards with the El Pilar project; as a group they were somewhat more disposed than other villagers to accept their fate. One of them, Don Vicente, took a philosophical view, telling me that any "mature country" had to have a nature reserve. He added that his fellow villagers were just not ready to understand the sacrifices citizens must make to develop a new nation.

However, in many interviews with a variety of villagers I heard the same story— farmers who had lost their land felt disillusioned. They reasoned that their support for Ford had resulted in the loss of their land. Some were especially outraged. Don Clemencio, who received far more compensation than the rest, BZ $3,000 (US $1,500) for land on which he had planted fruit trees, was nevertheless still furious, so much so that he loaded a rifle to prepare for taking a shot at Ford, although he never did. Another furious farmer told me that Ford should be returned to dust, in reference to sending her to her grave. He caught himself in the midst of a fit of rage, not at all consistent with the Evangelical Christian he had become; and then he quickly qualified his threatening statement with the clarification that his outburst represented the way he used to feel, and not how he felt at the moment. He added, "We are peaceful here in Belize, not like in Guatemala where she would be murdered."

Several years into the excavations, villagers began to see Ford differently, no longer giving her unqualified support as a benign protector dedicated to their interests. Instead they questioned if she was putting her personal benefits ahead of the welfare of the community. In a response consistent with Belizean skepticism about the motives of foreign archeologists, villagers jumped on the opportunity to make all kinds of wild accusations, spreading tall tales about Ford taking jade and other buried artifacts out of the earth and then enriching herself by selling them in the United States. Unfamiliar with the nonprofit financing required to support an archeological project, villagers assumed that it was a business venture designed to make money. They referred to the sites where Ford worked as "Anabel's Land" as if it were her personal acquisition, not that of the government. Although government officials did what they could to minimize Ford's damaged reputation, most villagers could not begin to understand that Ford was motivated by academic goals of discovery and education. Simply increasing the store of knowledge about Maya civilization did not seem to be a logical rationale for the investment of so much effort and money. Unfortunately, Ford's project fell into an undesirable category as the latest in a series of colonial intrusions by foreigners, which included the previous British and Spanish colonial occupations.

Ford's damaged reputation grew worse when villagers imagined bad luck coming from her presence. Criticisms of her escalated when female visitors from abroad swam in Chorro Creek, located not far from the El Pilar site. Maya legend held that women bathing in this water would cause the stream to dry up; and as luck would have it, the stream did dry up. Villagers had no reason to assume that the women committing the transgression were associated with Ford and they had no evidence to assume that the stream dried up immediately followed the swimming. Nevertheless, rumors of the event spread uncritically through the village, souring attitudes toward Anabel Ford.

Villagers' impressions of Ford being too single-minded about her work became enshrined in a story often repeated by Don Carlos, who claimed to have been at one time a dedicated Amigos member. During a walk in the nature reserve, he encountered a villager cutting down trees, a clear violation of policy and law protecting the nature reserve. Don Carlos did nothing to confront the violator because he feared getting shot. He reported to me that Ford reacted in anger to the incident, scolding Don Carlos for not taking action to save the trees. He then concluded that Ford cared more about the reserve than she did about human life; Don Carlos immediately left the Amigos group.

AMBIVALENCE TOWARD THE EL PILAR PROJECT[3]

From the Village

Despite low attendance at the Amigos meetings in the years 1997 and 1998, after the confiscation of farmers' land, a core group of about ten villagers remained unwilling to completely abandon the high hopes they had pinned on the El Pilar project. I learned about this group from the work of a community participation consultant hired after the establishment of the nature reserve to improve community relations. The University of Florida in Gainesville enabled Kevin Veach to work on the project, who at that time was a graduate student specializing in community relations. In a survey completed in 1997–98, Veach found that opinions in the community were not uniform, despite the obvious outrage expressed by some villagers.

Despite the fact that usually no more than ten to fifteen members would show up at meetings, many of the rest had adopted a "wait-and-see" attitude that Veach tried to encourage. This was evident when some of the farmers who lost their land planned to undo all of Ford's work by setting fire to the nature reserve. As news of this plan spread around the village, Veach organized 100 community members to oppose it. They signed a letter supporting Ford and put a stop to those who would turn to arson. Apparently, the regard for Ford and the tourism related possibilities were still on people's minds.

From a Partner Organization

Ford looked to build up sources outside the community for support, in one instance reaching out for the assistance of Elias Awe, director of Help for Progress, a not for profit organization (NGO) that managed grants from foreign donors. Help for Progress managed Ford Foundation (no relation to Anabel Ford) grants for activities associated with the El Pilar Project that supported Maya contributions to artisan work, crafts, farming, and other aspects of cultural heritage restoration. Awe was instrumental in marketing the concept of Ford's vision of what she called "eco-archaeology," a term adopted by Ford to evoke "the adventure of discovering the ancient culture of our natural world."[4] Awe appeared to be steady and strong in managing Ford's grant funds, though he mentioned to me that the style and structure of the operation always placed Ford clearly in control. He believed that his role in the project and the advice he gave to Ford were not as meaningful as he would have liked, particularly in providing a restraining influence on Ford's intense focus and drive.

From Government Sources

The Department of Archeology   Ford's relationship with the national government's Department of Archeology was uneven. On the one hand, she received its endorsement and support because staff members who were keenly aware of the need to develop archeological sites as a means to promote the flow of tourists into the country, because an increase in the number of tourists justified the departmental budget. Officially on August 6, 2001, the Acting Commissioner of the Department of Archeology released a statement professing unqualified loyalty to Ford's project, emphasizing the department's commitment to Bullet Tree Falls, the management of the archeological reserve, and the development of tourism. As a result, Ford had free rein to pursue her work.

On the other hand, the director of research, another high-ranking official in the Department of Archeology, was bent on exerting control and reining in Ford. A year and a half after she received the letter of unqualified support, Ford received another sternly worded letter, warning her that the Department of Archeology did not want to be held accountable for any mishaps resulting from her project, and that she should not saddle the Department of Archeology with obligations that would be difficult to fulfill, adding the thinly veiled threat that she was allowed to stay in the country for only a short time. An excerpt from the letter is provided here:

> It is not the responsibility of any archeological research to go into communities and make any unrealistic promises without consulting the Department of Archeology. All tourism-related plans must be synchronized with government development plans. As a guest researcher, you are in Belize for only a short period of time. After your research project leaves, the DOA [Department of Archeology] will have to deal with any potential problems that may have been created. Situations may not always be what they seem to be and therefore you should always contact the DOA before any decisions are made while you are working in Belize. We are held responsible for your project and therefore any actions on your part will impact the Department.[5]

Another high-level administrator in the Department of Archaeology also expressed serious questions regarding Ford's historical interpretation of El Pilar. He believed that the El Pilar over a thousand years earlier had been under great stress during a period of tremendous overpopulation and was far from representing either an idealized model of conservation or an example of a nature–culture nexus. His reasoning was as follows: at that time, the region now known as Belize had a population of at least one million, almost three times the number of people living in Belize in 2010. A population of this size would have placed unbearable demands on nearby forests to the point of complete deforestation. A pristine or extensive forest reserve would not likely have existed alongside a city-state, nor should it have been presented that way at El Pilar.[6]

I am ill equipped and unwilling to comment on the veracity of the apparent opposing points of view about the natural history of El Pilar, but it seems that Ford was committed to highlight conservation and nature, and not show off the monuments of high civilization. She took the step of putting monumental structures back underground, reburying them with the very earth that she had excavated. In other words, she "backfilled" the site, making sure that the soil was in place to help the forest recover and allow growing things—the forces of nature—to be the main features of the site, adding only a glimpse of a glorious past in the partial remains of monumental architecture. Her strategy to feature conservation made this official and other archeologists in the department particularly dismayed because of a lost opportunity to attract tourists.

Tourists in Belize gravitate toward spectacles, such as elaborate ceremonial centers where they can imagine ancient Maya priests, civil administrators, and astrologers strolling around plazas and courtyards, holding court for thousands of admirers. My experience on a trip to the El Pilar site resembled a walk in the woods. As an anthropologist, I appreciated the importance of learning about the natural world of ancient people, but I must admit I grew bored by the absence of architectural splendor. Between 2000 and 2004, tourist arrivals at El Pilar were a continuing hope and never a reality, averaging fewer than 1,000 people annually.[7]

Figure 2.4 Prime Minister Said Musa recognizing Anabel Ford's achievements.

From Government Officials

Strong verbal support for Ford came from the government and political leaders, such as Said Musa, the prime minister from 1998 to 2008 and head of the People's United Party (Figure 2.4), and his son Yasser, who took the lead in developing a new super-agency, the National Institute of Culture and History. The Institute brought together under the same bureaucracy the Institute of Archeology, the Institute of Creative Arts (headquartered at the Bliss Center Auditorium in Belize City), the Museum of Belize, the Houses of Culture, and the Institute for Social and Cultural Research. However, a potentially fruitful overlap between the El Pilar project and the Institute did not materialize.

In 2010, two years after a change in government marking the end of Said Musa's presidency, I drove to Belize City to speak with Yasser. Since he no longer held political office, I thought I could count on his being frank with me. I parked outside Yasser's new business building, an art gallery complex called The Image Factory. The upstairs resembled artsy stores in North American cities; only a Starbucks counter was missing. The downstairs contained a bookstore and modern art gallery.

I entered Yasser's office, a large space cluttered with books and papers scattered everywhere, similar to the typical appearance of a professor's workspace. The central piece of furniture was a drafting table, which held a pile of folders and some artwork. Yasser proved to be a lively conversationalist, eager to share his thoughts. He and his father wanted to see Belize become an international force for all the arts, both indigenous and modern. Many members of their political party reflected the values of progressive and liberal American culture—conservation, community participation, artisan work, indigenous culture, and grassroots development. Enthusiastic support came from Yasser and his father, Said Musa, who made the following pronouncement in the second week of June 2002.

> El Pilar brings together several innovative features on how we would like to see things develop in Belize in terms of inter-ministerial, inter-governmental and inter-community work for the benefit of the present generation. There is so much to be proud of our past, in our history; the greater Mayan civilization is still very much alive in Belize. It is not dead stones and ruins, but rather temples that should inspire us, a civilization from which we can learn many things. Conservation blended with bringing ideas about development paves the way for all arguments of contradiction between environmental concerns and development. The Government and people share the view that conservation, environmental protection and economic development are to bring about a better life for the people of today and for future generations (*Belize Times*, page 5, June 6, 2002).

Despite this high-minded rhetoric, the government's major investment in tourism was expansion of the harbor in Belize City to make way for large cruise ships. Records from the Belizean Tourism Board show that the visits due to the cruise ship traffic went from 48,116 in 2001 to 391,690 in 2002, a nine-fold increase made possible by the enlarged harbor. Between 2002 and 2004, the traffic again more than doubled. Meanwhile, the government provided little money to support the work at El Pilar, nothing much beyond paying the salaries of park rangers. The eight-mile trip by car from Bullet Tree Falls to El Pilar took at least 45 minutes, and often much longer. In the rainy season the road became muddy, slow, and almost impossible to navigate. In the dry season, rocks and bumps made for a very uncomfortable ride. Any serious effort to enhance the infrastructure necessary for the El Pilar project was not forthcoming during the administration of Said Musa. It was not until 2011 that the road became an all-weather road, 18 critical years after excavation had begun. El Pilar finally was within a 20-minute comfortable car ride, but by this time the site had established a reputation as being of little interest to tourists.

The government of Belize seemed equally indifferent to the security and personal safety of tourists. Again the appreciative rhetoric of the Prime Minister did not translate into the kind of security necessary for the development of tourism at El Pilar even though the U.S. Department of State issued a warning on June 27, 2002, barely two weeks after the Prime Minister's glowing speech.

> Robberies have been reported near the western border with Guatemala. In particular, criminals have targeted popular Mayan archeological sites in that region. Victims who resist when confronted by these armed assailants frequently suffer personal injury.

The Belizean government appeared not to have taken necessary action. Several months later, after Musa's enthusiastic expression of support, the consequences of inaction became a stark reality. Bandits crossing the Guatemalan border hijacked a tourist's car on the way to the archeological site. The intruders forced a driver and his son into the woods and then used the car to block the road, causing a jammed up line of cars that had no way to escape, either forward or backward.

The bi-weekly newspaper, *Amandala*, always ready to provide the details, reported on September 8, 2002, that one woman was repeatedly raped and 37 tourists were robbed. Such bad news hardly made El Pilar an attractive destination, especially with respect to San Ignacio tourism companies that specialized in transporting tourists to local sites of interest.

The Close of an Era

Although the robbery compounded already bad publicity, the prospects for tourism development at El Pilar were not wholly discouraging. During the first few years of the twenty-first century, the promise of a better future still hung in the air. Villagers appreciated the continuing project-related training and education they received in Maya crafts, organic farming, and tourism, hoping that this new knowledge and skill might empower them to develop a healthy tourism business. First the MacArthur Foundation, and then the Ford Foundation, brought in revenue for education and training, potentially leading to actual employment along with a small tourism boom. However, El Pilar never reached the level of a self-sustaining business enterprise without depending on periodic infusions of foundation money. Funding from the Ford Foundation from 1999 through 2003 kept hopes and some loyalty alive. Then when the money dried up, so did the following. As Anabel Ford reported it to me, the absence of ready money caused a comparable absence of interest among villagers. Ford separated from the community shortly afterwards, thus ending any lingering interest in what benefits might emerge from her leadership.

Don Beto was one of the last villagers to remain loyal to Ford. He was steadfast at her side until 2005, when a skirmish finished off their relationship. Both Ford and Don Beto gave me a similar account of how they parted ways at a celebration of the publication of her book on local nature and conservation. While Ford was engaged in a public presentation to promote this book for school use, Don Beto interrupted and, quite out of character, publicly lambasted her for charging money for the books. Stunned by the accusation, everyone, including Ford, was obviously taken aback. Several weeks earlier, while browsing in a San Ignacio bookstore, Don Beto had noticed Ford's book displayed for sale. He felt betrayed because previously he had received assurances from Ford that the book would be distributed free of charge to schoolchildren. Apparently Don Beto was unaware that the book also had to be sold commercially to adults to support its publishing costs.

The encounter ended any semblance of a constructive relationship between the two; however, it did not stop Don Beto and other villagers from picking up the pieces of the El Pilar project and putting them to work.

THE LEGACY OF THE EL PILAR PROJECT

After the definitive break between Ford and Don Beto, members of the Amigos group did not feel ready to give up completely on reviving Maya customs. Don Beto and the other 14 members of the group had bought into the idea, inadvertently championed by Ford, that Maya culture was a commodity that could be authenticated, exhibited, and marketed and for its own financial benefit. At a September 5th meeting in 2005, Don Beto announced that Ford was no longer a presence in Bullet Tree Falls and that from this point forward, members of Amigos would have to find their own sources of support and make the tourism project their own. Well positioned as its popularly elected president every year since 2000, Don Beto stood ready to take over and lead. He was everyone's choice, and he easily assumed the role of leader.

Taking a cue from Ford, the Amigos group under the leadership of Don Beto soon began its own search for international funding. Don Beto reached out to collaborate with Maria Garcia, an artisan specializing in ancient Maya crafts, who lived in the nearby village of San Antonio. Garcia's mission in her artisan work was similar to that of Don Beto, as a voice speaking to the world about an authentic Maya tradition. Garcia put Don Beto in touch with the Agroforestry Association,[8] a Nicaragua-based organization that managed grant funds provided by international donors.

Amigos submitted a successful proposal, and in 2007, received BZ $25,000 from the Agroforestry Association to start the Handicrafts Cooperative, consisting of village women trained to make and sell Maya-style pottery and peasant clothing. The funding enabled the purchase of sewing machines, lathes, tools, and the construction of an annex to the Cultural Center; and it provided expert training in the manufacture of pottery and clothing. That same year, Don Beto and his friend and contemporary Maya enthusiast Don Capo submitted another proposal to the Canadian Fund for Local Initiatives and obtained a grant of CA $18,000. Half of the funding was to finance the planting of seedlings in the El Pilar nature reserve and the other half to organize organic farming cooperatives.

In 2005, Don Epifanio, a member of the Mayan Way and a previous president of Amigos, reappeared on the local scene. Ten years after resigning from the Amigos group, he sought to fill a vacuum left by the departure of Ford. His attempt to dislodge Don Beto failed, but he still managed to maneuver Doña Betty out of her position as director of the Cultural Center. With Don Epifanio's encouragement, his daughter, an employee of the Belize Rural Development Programme, wrote and submitted a proposal to the Belize Rural Development Programme funded by the European Union to establish a workshop for jewelry and sculpture, using local woods, stones, seeds, and cow horns. As a result, the village received a grant of BZ $25,000.

The Amigos de El Pilar had learned their lessons well. During one of their meetings in 2009, I listened as members discussed what they should write into a proposal in order to justify funding for a project to teach village youth about local flora and fauna. With all the diligence of seasoned professionals, they "brainstormed" a number of suggestions: "the presence of an indigenous community," "the bounty of flora and fauna," "the emphasis on conservation," "the archeological sites," and "the active participation of women in cooperative organizations." As I was walking out with participants at the end of the meeting, I remarked that they had been promoting the same ideas for more than a decade. They agreed and complained that they could never get enough help from the outside world. One person bluntly asked, "Can you help us in Texas?" Others grunted in agreement. I realized that they had learned more than I had expected about how to exploit the value of cultural heritage as a commodity.

REFLECTIONS ON FORD AND STRATEGIES OF INTERVENTION

The mood of the politicians, government, and villagers was outwardly enthusiastic, but enthusiasm alone, often short lived, could not make for success. Ford spliced together and balanced many factors in attempting to make her project work: the villagers, the national government, land acquisition, the Department of Archeology, the tourists, and the donors. Despite Ford's attention to detail and strong determination, the odds were pretty high that something would go seriously wrong. Her overriding commitment to display Maya conservation and the nature–culture nexus proved to be her Achilles heel. Her focus on conservation did not attract tourists to the village; and when farmers lost their land to the government, their goodwill deteriorated. Also, she seems to have relied too much on the support of others, whose commitment was shallow, such as government officials who might have helped, but did not provide necessary transportation improvements and security infrastructure to support the project. The Department of Archaeology appeared to go along with Ford's agenda, The staff was committed to its mission of attracting tourists; consequently they were disappointed by the lack of attendance at El Pilar. Also, many of them disagreed with her interpretations of the consciously conservationist Maya past, especially in the height of the El Pilar accomplishment (600 A.D. to 1000 A.D.) when so much of the land is thought to have been overused and over-populated. Thus, they were not enthusiastic about encouraging her efforts. Apparently, it was financial support from international foundations that kept the project alive but this source of funding eventually dried up.

In acting as an agent of change, Ford was enmeshed in her own culture. She embodied the progressive ideals of American society when the counter-culture ruled in the 1960s and '70s, an era of respect for indigenous cultures, participatory community decision-making, and grassroots development. But it also was a time when many well-intentioned initiatives went awry because they were designed and implemented from the top down with insufficient cultural awareness. Perhaps a chorus of important people championing her cause and echoing her sentiments produced an inordinate amount of optimism and clouded a more realistic view of the challenges inherent in Ford's project.

Ford as Patrón

Although Ford was not in control of all the variables that might have led to greater success, she seemed to have brought troubles onto herself by unwittingly adopting the persona but not the behavior of a *patrón*, a historic and familiar role taken in

Latin America by landowners, managers, and employers who exercised authority over common laborers. In colonial times the role of the *patrón* was defined in the context of overseeing plantation operations, without the advantage of widespread literacy or a written contract. The *patrón* was a boss and benefactor who curried favor and appreciation by being attentive to personal, family, and community needs of poor peasants (*peones*) treated as clients. Present-day challenges inherent in carrying out the role of *patrón* are great, as one must be "on the ball" all the time, sensitive to people's needs, and norms of interaction. The *patrón* ideally responds to expressed needs and resolves tensions as they arise, such as in times of family illness or personal disagreements. The *patrón* also provides a bridge to ease conflict between social classes and acts as an intermediary to represent local clients in dealing with institutions and high-ranking leaders in the larger society. More specifically, the *patrón* may help to arrange to pay for legal contacts, medical care, education, and jobs for the offspring of clients, sometimes guiding children to a future that would otherwise be out of reach for poor peasants. In return, peasant laborers tend not to shirk their duties, while returning loyalty and sometimes affection to the *patrón*. These relationships are based on informal interpersonal transactions managed individually rather than collectively.

Anthropologists and other social scientists have extended the analytic category of "patron–client relations" to apply to peasant societies around the world, not limiting themselves to discussion of *patróns* and *peones* in Latin America. More broadly defined, patron–client relations refer to informal dyadic connections that tie people together across different social strata, occurring in such diverse locations as Southeast Asia, Afghanistan, Korea, and Poland, for example.[9]

In my own case, I have on occasion assumed the patron role in the patron–client paradigm. While working in Africa over the course of 16 years as a researcher and consultant for various divisions of the U.S. government and the World Bank, I always maintained close working ties with younger African colleagues who were highly skilled in interviewing, translation, and research. By virtue of my being their employer, and their lack of other employment opportunities, I became their patron. Our relationships were warm and personal, solidified by eating meals together and hanging out at each other's homes. We signed no formal contract about the work I expected from them, but they expected a lot from me, not just paying for their work, but also helping to resolve family problems, gain access to medical care, and establish connections with other foreigners who might point them toward future job opportunities.

The informal nature of our ties meant that we had no precise limits on mutual reciprocities, which had to be transacted over time and defined on a case-by-case basis. I always felt vulnerable because I might receive requests that I was incapable of fulfilling, thus creating the appearance that I was deliberately betraying my clients. I did not want them to regard me as a false friend, an unreliable patron unworthy of respect and loyalty.

An inconsistent path of transaction and expectations between Ford and others impeded the project. A *patrón* gives land to be worked, and would be expected to stand between farmers and a government that wanted to acquire farmland.

However, in this case, villagers formed the opinion that Ford had been a prime mover in the removal of the land, and they took it to mean that she did not embrace the *patrón's* role. In the ethnography of Latin America we learn that a confidant (*hombre de confianza*) is likely to emerge from among the *patrón's* followers. This confidant may offer advice based on an insider's perspective, and therefore become a key to a *patrón's* success. If Ford had pursued a more holistic approach, then the El Pilar project might have unfolded differently. If Don Beto and Don Elias had become valuable confidants, and unequivocally supported the goals of the project, they might have contributed to maintaining more harmonious relations with the villagers. If Ford had taken a more holistic approach, she might have been more open to alternative interpretations and public presentations of the past in consultation with her associate Elias Awe and with her colleagues in the Department of Archeology.

Ford's Legacy

Any disappointment that Ford may have had in Bullet Tree Falls did not dampen her enthusiasm for her mission, as she continued pursuing the same kind of work with a much smaller following in the nearby village of Santa Familia. There she turned her attention to introducing the topics of nature and conservation into primary school education, while funding small experimental efforts in organic gardening through her own foundation, called Exploring Solutions Past. Narciso Torres, whose family lost land in the creation of Ford's nature reserve, nevertheless joined with Ford in this effort; given the opportunity to earn some money, he was ready to forget the past.

In the short run, Ford's primary effect on the community was the commoditization of culture, where people had learned to organize themselves to apply for funds to invest in selling *onsite experiences* and souvenirs symbolic of their heritage. Although in this respect her legacy was quite different than what she had intended, she has had a potentially profound effect on a new generation too young to be employed in her project. Many young villagers attending Belizean high schools and universities began to pursue studies in business and tourism, learning independently about ecotourism and Ford's concept of eco-archeology. They were prepared for a future in which they could be the leaders in a viable tourist industry. The nature reserve, young villagers' knowledge of their cultural heritage, and the significance of their natural surroundings will not disappear.

Toward the end of my research, Anabel Ford was attracting interest again in Bullet Tree Falls, eight years after moving her activities to Santa Familia. Did villagers want her back? On February 26, 2013, several months after Don Beto's untimely death, I found the following message in my email account:

> Things are happening in BTF [Bullet Tree Falls], they want a fiesta, they want me to be involved, they want to increase members in AdEP (*Amigos*), and they want to improve Be Pukte [The Cultural Center].

Stating that she was "keeping aloof" and that one should not be too hasty in coming to conclusions, she inquired, "Where are you in the writing?" and then added, "There may be an epilogue."

It seems that villagers still wished for the vision and resources that a *patrón* might bring to them. With the passage of time and with Don Beto's death, their substitute *patrón*, no longer in the picture, they may have pushed negative feelings aside far enough to entertain a renewed and revamped relationship with Ford. When I was proofing the final pages of this book in October 2015, I checked in with Ford to find out how things were going. As she anticipated, there was a revived interest, and it came from the elementary school in Bullet Tree Falls and its principal. It does seem that she stimulated a continuing interest which will have an effect, most likely in school children and the effect will rest in an altered conception of their surroundings. In a subsequent email on Oct 31. 2015, Ford reported renewed interest in El Pilar project in the Department of Archeology and she is planning a celebration at the El Pilar site in the summer of 2016, commenting that "there are winds a changing!"

3/The Rastafarian Transformation[1]

It was a warm September night at the Mopan Bar when I met Charlie Samuels in a chance encounter that changed the focus of my fieldwork in Bullet Tree Falls. Entirely open with no walls, the bar's serving and storage area for beer and liquor invited my gaze as customers milled about, relaxing on chairs or stools, and occasionally stepping outside through a back exit to watch the river rushing by.

I had gone through the same routine at another bar many years earlier when I first set foot in Benque. If no alternative presents itself, a bar is a public space where total strangers may enter and begin meeting people. Generations of anthropologists before me have successfully employed this strategy. My attitude was that I would be pleased to meet anyone who seemed friendly. Charlie Samuels approached and caught my attention. He was about 40 years old, a Creole with much darker skin and fuller face than anyone else in the bar, distinctive also because of his flared nostrils and the beginnings of dreadlocks. I found him to be extremely outgoing, far friendlier than the others, and eager to make my acquaintance. Charlie spoke English well, which in itself was unusual in Spanish-speaking Bullet Tree Falls. My first thought was that his style and personality might be an individual aberration. Later in my research, I found many features of Charlie's appearance and extroverted style to be shared among other Creoles living in Bullet Tree Falls.

He showed definite signs of inebriation, though he managed to summon up an invitation to visit his home to meet his mother. I knew that when someone had too much to drink, it was a danger sign, but I convinced myself otherwise. How could anyone asking me to meet his mother be dangerous? My on-the-spot decision worked even much better than I had expected, as Charlie became my friend and field assistant, and I rented a room right there in his family's house.

We arrived at Charlie's home by walking several blocks down the road from the bar around 9 P.M., leaving only enough time for an introduction. His mother, of Maya heritage, was polite and curious, as I fielded the usual questions posed to foreigners. "How long would I be in the country?" "How did I like it?" "Did I feel welcomed?" I ended the conversation by asking for and receiving permission to return the following day to meet Charlie's father, who was of Creole background and had a family history in the area. The next day during our conversation Charlie's father flashed a mischievous grin, explaining that Charlie's mother was attracted to him because she "liked the Creole boys." Several days later I met Charlie's aunt Cecilia, who expressed her view that Creoles are much more amorous than the Mestizos.

This typecasting was consistent with what I found later about the self-cultivated identity of Creoles, who distinguish themselves from others as being more attractive, sociable, warm, and sexually desirable.

Charlie and his friends placed a high value on maintaining harmony and a sense of community among themselves, and they were quite ready to include Americans in their inner circle. Their perspectives in this regard derived from their recently imported Rastafarian culture that emphasizes social harmony and embraces people of all races. However, I had previously become aware of the long-term historical antagonism between the Creoles and Maya-Mestizos.[2] It showed up only now and then while I was working in the village, and was stronger in the past in the wake of political movements that advocated Creole militancy and separatism, especially in the 1920s and again in the late 1960s in the wake of the Black Power Movement. The counterbalancing of these two conflicting norms, harmony and antagonism, will be the subject of this chapter.

ETHNIC CONFLICT AND PROBLEMS OF HIERARCHY

Creoles in Bullet Tree Falls have always been in a unique position. At first they were privileged, landowning families. Charlie's great-great-grandfather, Benevolent Samuels, owned a three-mile stretch of land extending east from the Mopan River in Bullet Tree Falls to eventually include half of San Ignacio. He, a wealthy descendant of a Belizean–Creole union, was also a noted benefactor. He made donations of land to the Anglican and Catholic churches. His downfall came during a trip to Belize City, where he was involved in a poker game with a member of the Belizean gentry, a man by the name of Melhado. A bad poker hand and an unwise bet drove a drunken Benevolent into signing away most of his property. This transaction included all but 2,000 acres, which stayed in the family until the decade when Charlie was born. The 2,000 acres covered one-half of Bullet Tree Falls, starting east of the river, moving towards San Ignacio.

The Samuels family did not engage in farming; instead they rented plots of land to Maya-Mestizo farmers of the village. None of the Maya-Mestizo rules of patron–client relations applied, as the Samuels were distant, impersonal landlords, far from conforming to the ideal of benevolent patrons. Charlie's grandfather, Henry Samuels, administrated the family's farmlands, and according to Don Beto, his painfully strict style gained him a reputation as the most hated man in the village. His tenant farmers on milpas growing corn and other crops had no choice but to rent on a year-by-year basis, with no guarantees for future use rights. He forbade them from planting trees either for harvesting fruit or for producing lumber. If a renter broke the rules, the punishment was to be smacked with the flat side of Samuels's machete. Henry Samuels's behavior broke expected norms in other ways as well, such as habitually coming down to the river to bathe in the nude, a practice that especially offended the typically modest Maya-Mestizo women of the village.

Maya-Mestizo resentment against Creoles was not confined to the Samuels family alone; those with Maya heritage strongly believed that Belize was their

Figure 3.1 Creoles working the lumber trade—early twentieth century.

country, and that the status of Creoles as major landowners was illegitimate, any-where. It seemed obvious to Maya-Mestizos that the archaeological landmarks of ancient Maya civilization, covering the surface of most all of Belize, validated their claim to inherit the land. They regarded people of African ancestry as lateco-mers, having arrived in the eighteenth and nineteenth centuries to work in the lum-ber industry, at first as part of the system of slavery (See Figure 3.1). Maya-Mestizo contempt for Creoles could be quite personal. Charlie recalls being ridiculed as a child when adults called him "blackbird," and fellow students called him "negrito" (little black one). Villagers showed even greater contempt for Creoles whose appearance was too *"negro, negro,"* which translates as "black, very black," too dark to be acceptable to those of Maya or Mestizo origin. Maya-Mestizos claimed that Creoles were bolder, louder, more confident, and more audacious than "ordi-nary sensibilities would allow." Christian pastors added to the chorus of criticism, characterizing Creoles as too "licentious," unsuitable (and unwilling) to become "obedient servants of the lord."

Attitudes Toward the Garifuna

Mayan-Mestizo attitudes toward the Garifuna were similarly negative. The Garifuna were of African and Amerindian background, having migrated to Central America in the late eighteenth century; they spoke their own language and regarded them-selves as culturally different from Creoles. The Creoles, likewise, saw them as a separate people, but to the Maya-Mestizos, they all were of a common stock—black was black! Maya-Mestizos espoused a racist theory of behavior, believing that Blacks were by nature more inclined to engage in physical violence and unable to step away from a fight, in contrast to their own self-identified nature as more humble and far less confrontational.

Maya-Mestizos' contact with Garifuna provided villagers with more evidence to justify their racist point of view. The British colonial government brought Garifuna into the government workforce. The government viewed them as loyal servants to the Crown because they willingly learned English and proved themselves to be disciplined workers. They functioned well as intermediaries between the British and the Maya-Mestizo, without being so numerous as to present any threat to British rule. The British sent Garifuna to Bullet Tree Falls to serve as schoolteachers for village children.

Older Maya-Mestizos told me about their school days, recalling how frightened they were of the Garifuna teachers. Exhibiting airs of superiority, teachers made fun of Maya folklore, ridiculed stories about magical dwarves and frogs coming from the sky, and maligned Maya-Mestizo villagers for speaking what they called "inferior languages"—Spanish and Maya. They believed that English was the only worthwhile language, and enforced an English-only policy in the schools. As punishment for students who lapsed into Maya or Spanish, the teachers "brought out the lash."

Downward Mobility and Creole Resentment

In the late 1960s the Creoles of Bullet Tree Falls went from being landowners to being almost landless because of politically driven land reform that divided up landed estates and turned them over to Maya-Mestizos. The Honorable George Cadle Price, at the time the Belizean-born premier and head of the independence-minded People's United Party, oversaw the expropriation of land in a decade-long process. The land to be redistributed was once owned by British landlords and their descendants of mixed British and African Heritage, who identified as part of the Creole population. As a result of Price's efforts, landless rural populations (mostly Maya-Mestizos) became owners of 535,000 acres of land in Belize by the time of national independence in 1981.

Price's own background was mixed, an amalgam of the people of Belize—part Maya, part Mestizo, part African, part British. Not tied to any particular ethnic group or racially tinged worldview, he derived his personal philosophy from the Catholic paradigm of social justice. He did not intend to favor one group over another in implementing land reform; it just happened that in one part of Bullet Tree Falls those who owned land were the British and the offspring of Creole-British unions, meaning that the Maya-Mestizos gained at their expense. Despite Price's governing philosophy of inclusion, racial divisiveness worsened after land reform.

Before land redistribution, most of the 2,000 acres from Samuel's estate had been owned by Charlie's aunt, Cecilia Samuels, and her common law husband, Victor Cano. They lost most of this land, gaining back only a small portion through a petition that Victor submitted to the government. Victor and Cecilia were able to keep their home and 23 acres along the river, an area known as "The Peninsula" because it jutted out into the Mopan River dividing the village into two parts. Over time, part of this piece of land took on an identity as a Creole enclave dominated by Cecilia, Victor, their 13 children, and Cecilia's siblings. Offspring of this extended family constitute the core of the Creole population that has been living in the same area for several decades, building their houses, marrying others in their community, and continuing to harbor resentment toward Maya-Mestizos who wound up with the majority of the land.

To this day the Creoles have continued to vent their opposition toward Price and his political party, the People's United Party, for having redistributed their land. Since the 1960s, they have continued to support any political party that expressed opposition to the People's United Party. At first they supported the National Independence Party, and then the United Democratic Party, which had sought to maintain the colonial status of Belize; and after independence they were apt to undo Price's policy of wealth distribution. Instead, they promoted a nation that was far more pro-business than any arrangement conceived by Price.

As the losers in the land distribution program, Charlie Samuels and his cousins were prone to exchange belligerent insults aimed at the Maya-Mestizo, particularly when they were partying, drunk, or high on marijuana. They fumed and fussed about the "little Indians" and "the Spanish," pronouncing the words slowly with contempt. They derided the San Andrés Guatemalan refugees as the "White Ones," and referred to the patriarchs of this group as "Spanish Whities," with obvious disgust in their voices. Another Creole put-down for Maya-Mestizos was to call them "big-bellied Panias" (a derogatory term for Spaniards, meaning the Maya-Mestizos). Also, Creoles seemed uninhibited in their stereotypical belief that Maya-Mestizos smelled bad. If seated next to a Maya-Mestizo on the bus, a Creole would take another seat at the first opportunity, while muttering about the odor of "Indians." One of Charlie's female cousins, Aleida, reviled "the Spanish" not only for taking her land away, but also for selling the land once they had acquired it. There was a case of one family she identified as having had sold their land; I checked and confirmed that she was right. She did not name other families, and I could not find other examples of land resale.

The El Pilar project deepened the split between Maya-Mestizos and Creoles. The Creoles claimed that the "the Spanish" (that is, the Maya-Mestizo) did not really understand Anabel Ford, nor did they have any idea about how to relate to "the White World" she represented. Some Creoles commented to me that "the Spanish" chased out Ford because they could not get beyond their suspicions of White people, and were firmly of the opinion that Ford would have succeeded in bringing prosperity to Bullet Tree Falls if only "the Spanish" had let her complete her work.

CREOLES IN BELIZE CITY—IDEAS OF OPPOSITION

Historically, the national port of Belize City was dominated by Creoles working in the lumber industry, with Maya-Mestizos being only a small minority among urban residents. The concentration of Creoles in the city provided a crucible for the development of a distinctive ideology and cultural trends that continue to the present day. Historically Creoles regarded themselves as a class of exploited workers, they started to publicly express their frustrations in the early part of the twentieth century. They first rioted in 1917, to protest working conditions, and then again in 1919, in what was known as the "Ex-Serviceman's Riot," led by Creole soldiers returning from the Middle East theater of World War I, where they had suffered continuous racist insults from the British army officers who supervised their work. They experienced complete segregation—their platoon, their barracks, and their social life—and they received unequal treatment in pay, rations, and medical care. After they finished their term of service, the British refused to hand over their final paychecks and forced them to arrange their own transportation to Belize from war-time stations in Europe and the Middle East.[3]

The riot was pure revenge. Soldiers broke into the houses of merchants, targeting British Whites and the "near Whites" (Creoles). The rioting soldiers yelled, "These are brutes, we do not want them here!" "This is our country and we want to get the White man out!" and "We are going to kill the White sons of bitches tonight ... this is a Black man's night!" (Shoman 2010: 57).

Rising Creole Status

In later decades a substantial segment of the Creole population was ready to embrace activist messages about recompense and social justice. One messenger or agent of change was Evan X. Hyde, who went back to his home country, Belize, in 1968, after graduating *magna cum laude* from Dartmouth College, ready to change the world and make life better for Creoles. His intention was to bring the American Black Power agenda of the 1960s home to Belize. His years at Dartmouth did not make him a typical elitist Ivy League graduate. Instead he became a militant Black with a big Afro haircut, emulating the style of dissident Black leaders in the United States, such as Floyd McKissick, Stokely Carmichael, and Malcolm X, whose vision of Black Power provided a blueprint for action in combating racial oppression and building Black institutions in education, health care, and politics. Hyde wanted to construct a similar program of action for Belize, and for that purpose established the United Black Association for Development (UBAD).

Hyde's Black Power stance led to his calling Belize's mixed race Premier George Price a "Mayan racist."[4] During the 1970s, Hyde's view (later recanted) was that Price was eager to facilitate the advancement of Maya and Mestizo peoples, but not Blacks. He was upset about Price's plans to move the capital inland, away from Belize City, ostensibly because it had been nearly destroyed by Hurricane Hattie in 1961. His complaint was that Price had no plans to rebuild Belize City's South Side, home to the mostly impoverished Creole population, but instead planned to relocate the capital to a place that was to be called "Belmopan," resting on land historically recognized as the heart of Maya civilization. Worse still, from Hyde's perspective, the proposed design of government buildings mimicked the architecture of the Maya ruins, where power and authority emanated from the temples, priestly residences, and plazas, with wide expanses of steps cascading from the buildings and descending to public plazas. In Hyde's view, this BZ $20 million project was clear evidence of Price's favoritism toward the Maya and disregard for Creoles.

Opposition to Black-White Alliance

Hyde attacked what he saw as a major cultural myth perpetuated in schoolbooks and everywhere else in public life—the notion of unity and harmony between Blacks and Whites. The proof of racial togetherness was represented in historical memory about the country's supposed finest hour, when White and Black Belizeans, masters and slaves, arm-in-arm, finally repelled the Spanish once and for all in the 1798 Battle of St. George's. According to legend, British sovereignty won the day thanks to the cooperation of slave and master. Once a year, on September 10, the entire country celebrates the victory with parties, fireworks, new flags, stick-on flag tattoos, and lots of drinking. Hyde called the tale "brilliant historical propaganda" and "a legitimization of the Creole bourgeoisie's supremacy in civil service administration."[5]

Hyde's task was daunting, as the impression of unity between Black and White was everywhere in the country—on plaques, pictures, and lapel buttons. Even the middle of the Belizean flag displays the message of unity in the form of two shirtless men, one White, the other Black; the first holds an ax to cut logs and the second holds a paddle to guide the raft downriver (Figure 3.2). The duo appear bonded and heroic in building the economic might of the country.

Reviving Marcus Garvey

Part of Hyde's inspiration was to make his politics a continuation of Marcus Garvey's "Black Power" efforts earlier in the century. Born in Jamaica in 1887,

© Andrew Gordon

Figure 3.2 Symbol of Belizean unity on the national flag and everywhere.

Garvey became a leading intellectual Black activist in the early twentieth century, as a worldwide voice for justice and dignity for people of African descent. He initially learned the skill of militant messaging in Jamaica, and then traveled in Europe for self-education, meeting with as many European leaders as possible. In 1916, he made New York City the headquarters of his Universal Negro Improvement Association (UNIA), dedicated to supporting Black enterprise, with branch offices in 101 countries throughout the world. In New York City, he founded the Negro Factories Corporation, which included grocery stores, restaurants, cleaners, and publishers. He also established a shipping line with three commercial ships intended for transporting the descendants of Africans back to Africa. In 1920, at the age of 33, already worldly and eloquent, Garvey travelled to Belize at a time when Creoles were angry and rebellious. Garvey exhorted Black Belizeans (Creoles) to take action to right the wrongs inflicted on them. Garvey's visit to Belize was an obvious success, as he was well received for his spellbinding speeches and inspirational ideas, which led Belizeans to establish a chapter of the UNIA and build a three-story structure to house the organization, modeled after Garvey's headquarters, Liberty Hall in New York.[6]

However, the political energy and the confrontational style left in Garvey's wake subsequently dissipated. Just nine years after his visit to Belize, the UNIA became known as a "Friendly Society," a name that stands for a fraternal betterment organization. When Garvey returned to Belize in 1929, his demeanor was reported to have been "very moderate in every way." He had become conciliatory, "careful to avoid any expression to which any exception could be taken."[7]

Afterwards, Liberty Hall in Belize City was periodically left vacant and sometimes rented to other civic and to educational groups. During the 1930s, Liberty Hall again became the center of political activity, when the labor movement used it as a place to hold meetings. Today, a small group of Rastafarian youth affiliated with the UNIA use the space for artisan work. Otherwise Liberty Hall remains mostly unused, with the exception of occasional meetings of a civic group known as the Central American Black Organization.

Upon returning from Dartmouth, Hyde's strategy was to share his political message with a handful of still faithful members of Garvey's UNIA. Finding Hyde to be too radical, they wanted nothing to do with him. It was at that moment that Hyde decided to establish his own organization, the United Black Association for Development (UBAD). The UBAD gained political power by recruiting two rising political activists who happened not to be of African descent but nevertheless sympathized with the oppression of Creoles. One was Assad Shoman who later became a leading figure in the Belizean government. The other was Said Musa, who eventually became Prime Minister. Despite attracting a close-knit group of loyal followers, Hyde could not expand his support. He was soon to discover the limited tolerance of Belizeans for confrontation politics and their noticeable tendency to avoid organized political conflict in addressing the issue of racial divisions.

In 1974, Hyde tried his hand at politics, running for legislative district office representing his own political party UBAD, but his efforts netted only 89 votes.

Neither Garvey nor Hyde really understood the non-confrontational nature of Belizeans and how impossible it was for the Creole population to maintain a combat-
ive, separatist stance. Divisions based on color were not compatible with the way
people perceived each other. Those who were darker-skinned did not necessarily
see a rigid distinction between themselves and those who were lighter-skinned.
Then and now, a full spectrum of color and appearance is acceptable in Belize,
even occurring in the same family, from dark to "near White."

Evan X. Hyde's Afro-Centrism

Hyde's influence was of a cultural, not a political nature, fostering a sense of
uniqueness and dignity among the people of African heritage. After his failed
foray into politics, he declared that the people had spoken and turned his attention
elsewhere. In August of 1969, he began extensive distribution of *The Amandala*, a
publication that had served as the mouthpiece of the United Black Association for
Development (UBAD). The term "Amandala" comes from the word *Amandla*,
which means, "power" in Xhosa/Zulu. Later, Hyde changed the content of *The
Amandala* to include national news, and it became the most popular newspaper in
Belize, published twice a week. In 1989, Hyde founded the first privately owned
radio station in Belize, and in 2004, he established a television station, in both
instances using the media platform to promote the recognition of Belize's African
past as part of his Afrocentric cultural agenda.

Hyde remarked to me personally that he ultimately prevailed, despite his unsuc-
cessful efforts in electoral politics, because he helped change the perception of
Creoles about themselves, giving them a sense of uniqueness and pride. The
Provost of the University of Belize, Angel Cal, pointed out to me that without
Hyde and his message of ethnic affirmation, neither African Studies nor Maya
Studies would have gained any footing in Belize. Hyde made the subject of ethnic
difference a respectable and legitimate topic for academic exploration.

As a strong and relentless defender of the rights of his people, he kept the
offices for his newspaper and radio station located among Creoles in the South
Side of Belize City. Nevertheless, he knew what was going on, and recognized
the desperation and rage that continued in certain Creole neighborhoods. Hyde
was careful to warn me, a White foreigner, not to walk the streets nearby his office
even in midday; and when I left his office, he accompanied me to the street and
quickly found me a taxi.

IDEAS OF HARMONY

In Hyde's memoir, *X Communications*, he recalls the time when his political
party, the United Black Association for Development (UBAD), was heading in a
direction that was not conducive to bringing about political change. Black activists
were trading in their separatist political identity for a more glamorous image
derived from popular culture, redefining what it meant to be of African descent.

Once politically motivated members of the party now seemed more disposed to maintaining a popularized "African-American" image, parading around with dashikis, sandals, and Afros in an attempt to mimic African style.[8]

A cultural revolution was percolating among Creoles in the 1970s, led by returned, educated youth, who had studied in Jamaica with the support of international scholarships. They projected a different style of being Black, one that was founded on Afrocentric culture and embraced new musical forms from Jamaica—a recently independent country, almost wholly Black, and brimming with cultural energy. One of the returned educated youth, Dean Barrow, gained prominence as a deejay and was a key player in this scene. Recently he has served as Prime Minister of Belize, his term of office extending from 2008 to 2016.

New Afro-Caribbean music trends caught fire, including calypso, which featured conga drums and guitars, and mento, a Jamaican form of calypso characterized by a rock-steady beat; it was relatively slow and was accompanied by pronounced, sensual dance steps. As mento receded in popularity, the blaring horns of circus-like ska music replaced it, later to be eclipsed by reggae, which ushered in a major cultural change in Belize.

Creoles who had studied abroad and those who had stayed at home shared in the cultural revitalization of the African Diaspora, taking it upon themselves to refashion the character of Creole life in Belize. They shaped a new image for the Creole generation entering adulthood in the 1970s, in stark contrast to their parents some of whom had been brought up to be model British subjects, well dressed and tidy, with a careful and unimposing presence. It was time for a change. The new generation wanted to project a style showing off their higher level of education and sophistication. Men rejected the tightly controlled presentation of self that was associated with the straight-ahead, disciplined walk of some of their colonial servant fathers, notably keeping buttocks pressed together. The new style of movement was what they called "the flop," in which walking consisted of one foot kicking in front of another to suggest an easy-going stride. They even dared to bring off-beat hairstyles and dress to their civil service jobs, copying images of African fashion and the personae of Rastafarians and Bob Marley.

Bob Marley's Message

Reggae music gained popularity in Belize City in the 1970s and '80s, eventually making its way to Bullet Tree Falls. Its distinctive double strumming of the guitar was fused with a danceable big-band sound. Musicians communicated the words and ideas of the Rastafarian faith through their reggae songs, especially those of the famous Jamaican singer Bob Marley.

Marley never personally travelled to Belize, but his message arrived through the radio and recordings infused with themes of peace, love, and harmony—basic features of the Rastafarian faith. His songs emphasized the oneness of humanity, the reverence for land, the promise of children, the means to talk to "Jah" (the word for God in Rastafarian religion), and, as one song goes, how to "stand up for your rights."[9]

Marley's first major-label reggae album, *Catch a Fire,* was released in 1973. His message was distinctively captured in the song "One Love," made famous in a later album Exodus, published in 1977. It became an anthem of the Rastafarian faith in Africa, America, Asia, Europe, and Belize. Its refrain is familiar in popular culture worldwide:

One love! One heart!
Let's get together and feel all right
Hear the children crying "One love"
Hear the children crying "One heart"

Saying, "Give thanks and praise to the Lord and I will feel all right."
Saying, "Let's get together and feel all right."

The Rastafarian creed, in its expression through Marley, was neither Black nor White. Chris Blackwell, Marley's manager, set the stage for Marley's international fame by extending reggae's appeal, not only to residents of the Caribbean, but also to White Americans and Europeans. Soon it spread to the rest of the world. Blackwell made sure Marley's music progressed beyond rustic Jamaican reggae; he turbocharged the sound with the dance beat of disco and the Motown sound of the 1960s and early 1970s. The music resonated with three or four guitar lines, accompanied by powerful syncopated drumming, sometimes with two drums, as well as call-and-response lyrics.

On that first 1973 major-label album, Blackwell dubbed the sound of a White guitarist, Wayne Perkins, onto tracks created by Marley and his group, The Wailers. Perkins was a "good old boy from Alabama," but Marley liked his work. After being thanked by Marley for his contribution to the album, Perkins commented on the difficulty in verbal communication. He said, "I'm from the South, you're from the islands, but when the tape rolls, we're communicating."

Marley himself was a racial synthesis of a Black mother and White father, what Jamaicans called a "Redman." His features were chiseled in a way that suggested European heritage, while his skin was obviously darker than his father's pale English tones; still lighter than other Jamaicans but with a reddish hue. Marley's embrace of mixed-race heritage was also exemplified by his very public affair with the Miss World winner in 1976, Cindy Breakspeare, the daughter of a Canadian mother and a Black Jamaican father.

Crack Takes Over

Marley, reggae, and Rastafarians became a widespread and important part of life in Belize City's South Side, lasting until 1984, when a new scene began to take over. A brisk cocaine trade was working its way north from South America at the same time a crack epidemic was devastating Los Angeles and other places in the United States, rural towns included. The drug trade brought troubles to Belize City when it became a pass-through venue for drugs being shipped north by plane and boat.[10]

Two problems occur when a country becomes an artery for international drug traffic. First, some of the transported drugs find their way into the domestic market, meaning that what was originally an American problem of crack addiction became a problem of crack addiction in Belize City. The second problem is the rise of gangs in charge of the drug trade, always ready to commit murder against competitors, which was a common occurrence right up to and including the time of my fieldwork. *Ganja* (the Jamaican word of Sanskrit origin for marijuana) was already in widespread use and a common part of life in Belize City in the 1970s and early '80s. By 1984, however, *ganja* was laced with a little crack cocaine, then a little more, and then a lot more. Ultimately, users bypassed marijuana altogether and went straight for the crack.

Escape to Caye Caulker

In the mid-1980s, some Rastas (the short form for Rastafarians) left Belize City because they wanted nothing to do with the cocaine scene. They sought refuge on Caye Caulker, an offshore island that became a headquarters for Rastafarian-and-*ganja*-seeking tourists. Anthropologist Anne Sutherland's 1998 book on Belize describes Caye Caulker at that time as a place for "young White tourists from Europe and the United States [who] seem to have an endless fascination with the exotic dreadlocked Rastas and reggae music—especially the words and music of Bob Marley, who is constantly quoted on Caye Caulker" (1998: 114). International travel guidebooks added to the buzz, one highlighting the island and its "open-air reggae club [with] dancing around a wood fire."[11]

Caye Caulker became a tourist haven—a hot spot for sun, surf, and parties—and an international playground for tourists, many of whom wanted to experience the pleasures of *ganja* and pursue amorous adventures. Rasta men in particular became a magnet for female tourists. Peace and love seemed to prevail, but for just a short time, as they were soon disrupted by crack and violence spilling over from Belize City.

A New Cultural Scene in Bullet Tree Falls

Henry Coleman, a Creole artist and Rastafarian advocate who was part of the *ganja* scene in Caye Caulker, was a magnet for tourists who flocked to his unusual studio, a tree house, where he both preached his faith and hung canvases in the tree to cultivate his own "scene" of artistic creativity. In 1990, a chance meeting occurred that brought Henry together with another artist, Charles Cano, brother of Victor Cano of Bullet Tree Falls, the one who came to be the landowner of the Peninsula. The result of this meeting was to change the lives of Creoles living in the village. At the time, Henry complained to Charles about the hostile atmosphere brought by crack cocaine on Caye Caulker—"too much paranoia, too much violence," he said. Charles told Henry about the green hills near Bullet Tree Falls, the pristine river for bathing, and the overall peaceful setting. Henry went to Bullet Tree Falls in late September 1991 to see it for himself, and he quickly fell in love with the place. His first contact was Victor Cano, who offered Henry a lease for a plot of land on the Peninsula where he could construct a house and garden. (See Figure 3.3 for a map of the Creole and Rastafarian Presence.)

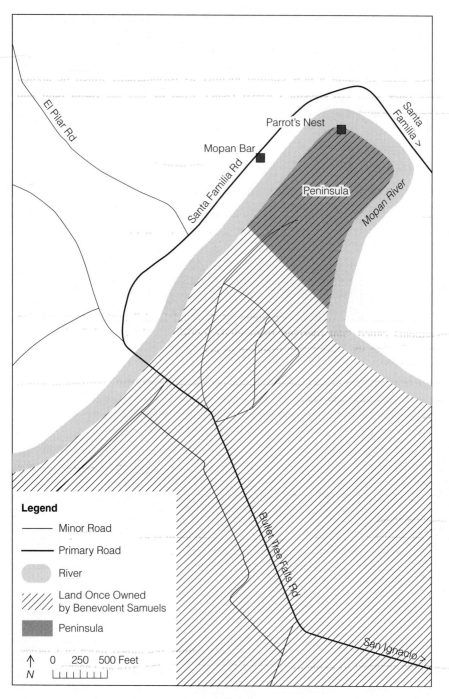

Figure 3.3 Village center—Creole and Rastafarian presence.

RASTAFARIAN AND CREOLE PRESENCE

After moving to Bullet Tree Falls, Henry Coleman soon acquired a loyal following for his Rasta teachings among the younger members in the Samuels family. He wanted them to adopt a new cultural identity as Rastafarians, which he argued would raise their self-esteem. I asked Henry what he and his Rasta faith had brought to Bullet Tree Falls. He answered in a slow and deliberate way, never hurried:

> The lifestyle that I was bringing to them was something new to them. I was bringing to them what you call extreme kindness, and love and respect. Not only in the word, but in the works and the action. And I was bringing to them humbleness, humbleness and lowliness. I was bringing to them high things.

He stretched out some words like "lowliness" in a bass tone for emphasis, broke up the word "humbleness" by enunciating each syllable separately, and pronounced "things" as "tings," in a mix of Creole and the Rasta style to signal his high level of spirituality. In preaching and teaching the principles of Rasta philosophy, Henry encouraged his followers to read and discuss the Bible. He described himself as "obsessed" by the need to feed others—just as Jesus would do, he told me. He served his followers rich stews of "ground foods" containing vegetarian ingredients called "ital (derived from vital) foods" mostly ground foods or root crops reflecting the Rastafarian mandate to get back to nature and free themselves of the contaminants of civilization found in packaged foods. The spiritual mandate for Rastafarians was to stay apart from the decadence of modern civilization, which they referred to as "Babylon."

Henry also brought to his followers another way of being Christian in a community that was historically Catholic but had moved toward Protestant Evangelical affiliations. Rastafarianism was certainly a kind of Christian faith and lifestyle, yet sharply distinguished from other forms of Christianity, because Rastafarians contend that the second coming of the Messiah already happened, as manifest in the person of Ethiopian Emperor Haile Selassie (1892–1975), also called Ras Taferi—with *ras* meaning head and *teferi* being the one who is feared. Thus, they felt no need to wait for Christ's return, believing that Heaven on earth is possible in the present.

HARMONY IN BULLET TREE FALLS

Elsewhere in the village, young people with Guatemalan Black Spanish roots (many from San Benito) also began to embrace their African origins. Previously they had not questioned why their physical features resembled those of Creoles, not being inclined to explicitly connect themselves to the African Diaspora. After Henry Coleman made his mark in the village, they, too, embraced a Rastafarian identity along with their African heritage. Like their Creole "brethren" (as Rastas would say), they expressed solidarity by greeting each other with the term "Ras."

A new generation with a greater measure of cultural pride emerged in the early 1990s, as evident in a soccer match between the boys of Bullet Tree Falls and the village of Succotz. The Bullet Tree Falls soccer team was composed of Creoles mostly from the Samuels family, who called their team Roots, a reference to Alex Haley's (1976) famous book and made-for-television miniseries of the 1970s, documenting the history of the African Diaspora in America from the beginnings of slavery to the present. Breaking out of an old cultural mold, the players from Bullet Tree Falls sported dreadlocks in a proud public display of their Rasta and African identity.

The Succotz team, made up of Maya-Mestizos, also decided to snub convention and make their ethnic identity a matter of pride, not shame. They wore their hair in ponytails in what they considered to be an "Indian style," an obvious contrast to the dreadlocks of the Roots team. No longer ashamed to recognize their Maya background, the Succotz team called themselves the Apaches, a name customarily used by outsiders, and particularly those living in Benque, to humiliate Succotz villagers. The Benque dwellers ridiculed their neighbors in Succotz for being backward and still speaking the Mayan language, a practice abandoned several decades earlier in Benque. The name Apache came from the depiction of savage Indians they would see on television in old American Old-West movies. These young soccer players of Succotz, like those of Bullet Tree Falls, chose to be audacious. It was the Apaches against the Roots, not a hostile affair and certainly far less competitive than it might have been in earlier times. Both teams lit up *ganja* before the match and competed with freewheeling fellowship and abandon.

Although these spiritually enlightened Creoles still felt some negativity toward Maya-Mestizos living in their own village, their new Rastafarian perspective prevailed, and they began to recognize that injustices had been inflicted on both groups by their British and Spanish colonizers. By accepting the legitimacy of ethnic diversity, they could see that they had common interests and concerns that brought them together to stand up for themselves in dealing with the depredations heaped on them by the outside world.

I reached a deeper understanding of the essence of Rastafarian identity in viewing a photo of a homemade recording session and simultaneously listening to the music. Charlie was playing guitar; his hair was long and shaggy, with dreadlocks in the making. His friend Harold, a mixture of mostly Maya-Mestizo and a little Creole, with a similar hairstyle, accompanied him on the guitar, as they pounded out songs to a reggae beat. Written in the Creole language, the lyrics described the arrival of the Spanish and expressed indignation at the ill treatment experienced by the Maya people. They picked up on Bob Marley's continual exhortation to "stand up for your rights," The song recorded by Charlie and Harold goes as follows:

Columbus, Columbus, Columbus
Fir Mi di ya long before Columbus
(*Translation*: Fire was here long before Columbus)
Mayas mi di ay long before Columbus
(*Translation*: Mayas were here long before Columbus)
Columbus, Columbus, Columbus
Come bust us

THE WHITE WORLD AND ROMANCE TOURISM

Creole Rastafarians reached out with their message of unity not just to Maya-Mestizos but also to foreigners, paying particular attention to White female tourists from North America and Europe. Local Rastas (Figure 3.4) learned what their counterparts discovered previously in Caye Caulker—being Rasta was sexy and appealing. After he had fully grown his dreadlocks, Charlie discovered that the female students who came to work on excavations at El Pilar expressed far more interest in him. He told me how his "dreads" assured him a different girlfriend every summer. Creole men with dreadlocks soon became an attraction for female tourists coming through San Ignacio to Bullet Tree Falls. Barbeques, *ganja*, booze, and romance enlivened the scene. (In Bullet Tree Falls the Creoles were not entirely faithful to the Rasta principle of avoiding alcohol.)

Some Creole villagers were especially adept at mixing socially with visiting tourists. Roberto, son of Victor Cano, was always in one dalliance or another with a female tourist, and sometimes with several at one time. During my fieldwork, Roberto often travelled to England to spend time with a female partner he first met when she came to Bullet Tree Falls as a tourist. In describing his experience being a Rasta in England, Roberto said, "They treat me like a rock star."

Some tourists who already knew about the Rasta scene quite directly sought it out. Raymond, a tour guide based on San Ignacio, told me that he frequently encountered young women in their late teens to twenties, wearing shirts that bore the phrase "I love Rasta." After one tour, he found a travel journal that a female passenger had left behind in his company's microbus; it listed three travel

Figure 3.4 Rastas hanging out in the tourist section of San Ignacio.

goals: "go to Tikal (a major Maya site in Guatemala), go to the beach, and experience a Rasta man." Raymond was an excellent resource for learning about romantic liaisons because he was a star in this line of work, perfectly cast for his leading role—soft-spoken, a little shy, and boyish, a good listener, in good physical shape, and a noted caver (spelunker). He told me about many international trips he had taken while having all of his expenses paid by tourist girlfriends, the destinations including New Mexico, Pittsburgh, Hawaii, and elsewhere in the United States. Raymond was not the only local man to travel, but he managed to find more opportunities than others. He told me that it was not unusual for women to initiate alliances by offering gifts consisting of items not easy to purchase in Belize, "gadgets like cell phones, laptops, and iPods."

The new Rastafarian subculture became part of the local scenery of San Ignacio. During the day, the Maya presence was dominant in San Ignacio, with minibuses transporting tourists to nearby archeology sites, whereas at night it was a Rastafarian scene punctuated by drummers who performed at the entrance to Mayawalk, the premier local touring company. Garan Lyles and Kimberlee Schluter, students in my field school, reported to me that the Rasta men of San Ignacio often became confidants, companions, and guides to female tourists. Their first encounters usually happened in a bar or restaurant and tended to end up in the tourist's hotel room. After a night out, the men, most of them friends, would compare notes on how well things were going in terms of gaining material benefits, which women happened to be paired up with which men, and how long the relationship might endure. After a girlfriend left the town, her suitor would again be on the lookout for another female tourist. Garan described these men as "lost boys" without a clear future, getting by as a result of "scoring" with generous women.

The Creoles in Bullet Tree Falls and San Ignacio fit into a broader pattern of romance tourism. In 2006, Jeannette Belliveau published an entertaining and seemingly credible encyclopedia of women seeking sex as tourists, under the catchy title *Romance on the Road: Travelling Women Who Love Foreign Men*. Using a variety of sources, she estimated that every year 600,000 women worldwide cross over geographical and cultural boundaries to explore romantic liaisons, often connected with a planned vacation.

I do not mean to imply that all female tourists in Belize were looking for an affair with a Belizean Rasta; nor do I wish to imply that all of the relationships formed by Rastas were not mutually affectionate and truly loving. I should point out, however, that the interest of female tourists in temporary liaisons was strong enough to keep 30 to 40 men in Bullet Tree Falls and San Ignacio well occupied, each man engaged in such activity several nights a week. In the village of Bullet Tree Falls, Rasta men regularly formed an ad hoc welcoming committee, inviting visitors to barbeques and parties, and introducing them to their culture of celebration, harmony, and *ganja*. Visitors, in turn, altered the attitudes and habits of villagers, teaching them a polite style of socializing without the use of foul language. Roberto told me how a girlfriend prompted him to speak more politely: "I used to use the F-word in every other sentence. She taught me that it was bad for their business of taking tourists out in the wilds on horseback."

The obvious inequality in financial wealth and flow of benefits from tourists to hosts did not seem to have presented any serious problem for the women who became benefactors. I spoke with one American woman who had invested a considerable amount of time with a man from the Samuels family. She claimed to feel real affection for this man, and she believed that he had the same feeling for her. She was well aware of the utility she brought into his life, honoring his requests for money without resentment and providing him with periodic gifts that cemented their relationship. To her, the arrangement was no more than a way to even out the accident of birth—she having been born in a wealthy country, and he having been born in a poor country.

After turning 40, Charlie had become a senior member of the Rasta men's welcoming committee. His American girlfriend in 2011 was a retired schoolteacher about 20 years his senior. During her relationship with Charlie, she bought a piece of land in Bullet Tree Falls, as did her two daughters, both of them finding their own Rasta companions. She kept up with Charlie by sending him gifts and intermittently flying to Belize from her home in Wisconsin, never with prior notice, just showing up when she pleased. She provided financial support that reinforced Charlie's commitment to being Rasta. One day at Charlie's home, I noticed a gift package that his benefactor had mailed to him; it included a poster of Bob Marley and a blue jeans jacket of the kind popular in the 1980s. Six months later, their relationship seemed to have run its course, romantically at least. However, Charlie continued to meet his interpersonal obligations, with obvious financial benefits, by arranging to put her village land up for sale.

A Note on AIDS

I was interested in how the Rasta men dealt with the threat of AIDS, perhaps because I personally would have felt very nervous about having casual sex with strangers. In the late 1980s and 90s, AIDS was a quick and certain killer, not the manageable disease it has now become for many, but not all. After listening to Raymond candidly describe the free-flowing, unfettered sexual practices of men, I asked him about tourists' attitudes toward condoms. He replied that only rarely did tourists ask for protection and only rarely did the men use it. He continued with a story about an international team of health specialists who had come to San Ignacio to provide AIDS education and distribute condoms. Raymond claimed to have had sexual relations with two of the women health workers on the team, and in neither case did they request the use of a condom. He added any concern about condom use was no different, at all, for the female doctor and the female nurse with whom he had relations.

I wondered if the men were at all cautious about staying free of HIV infection. Raymond said that they were wary, but only in a somewhat extraordinary way, at least from my viewpoint. The men judged the likelihood of a woman being HIV-infected by her travel history. Raymond provided an example, "If she's been to Caye Caulker first, then it is best to keep your distance. Caye Caulker is known for diseases." No longer part of this "dating scene," Juan, one of Raymond's friends, now describes himself as a survivor for not having died of AIDS.

Gentrification

Beginning in the 1990s, increasing numbers of North Americans looked to Mexico and Central America for vacation destinations with ecologically minded themes and a free-spirited lifestyle. At that time the main attractions for those who sought an uncomplicated, back-to-nature lifestyle in Bullet Tree Falls were Fred Prost's resorts, comprising one complex of guest cottages and another of cabins built into trees, called the "Parrot's Nest," designed to simulate a life experience nestled in the canopy of the tropical rain forest. Prost, the developer, had formed a friendship with Henry Coleman in Caye Caulker, and copied his friend's style of housing his art studio in the trees so he constructed his resort in the treetops of the Rasta-Creole Peninsula. An American woman from Montana married and became a business partner of another Rasta-minded son of Victor Cano. This couple built a guesthouse on another plot of Peninsula land, intending to cater to tourists with ecological sensibilities. They constructed the building to blend in with the forest and served natural food to guests. Bullet Tree Falls soon gained a reputation as an "in" place for tourists, due to visitors from faraway places praising the beauty of the setting and the freedom of interaction with villagers. Several North American visitors who ended up staying for longer periods of time remarked that they were strongly attracted by "the magic" of the place and its "hippie vibe."

By the year 2000, some North Americans and a few Europeans who came to Bullet Tree Falls began searching to find lots on which to build retirement homes and second homes. As buyers, they experienced no resistance to their plans to settle in the village. In 2012, about 100 North Americans and Europeans owned property or had taken up residence in and around the village. Local hosts projected openness to outsiders, and the low cost of living resembled famous artistic and countercultural-type communities before grossly inflated prices made life so much more expensive. Examples in the United States include Taos, New Mexico; Provincetown, Massachusetts; Sedona, Arizona; and Venice Beach, California. Rastafarianism and the message of oneness and harmony paved the way for new settlers, and, as in the previously mentioned U.S. communities, initiated a process of gentrification in the construction of upscale housing. Foreigners bought into what they described as their "piece of paradise," paying for land way beyond the local price—one of them for example, purchasing a piece of property along the riverfront for US $125,000, a thousand times greater than the price the seller would have paid for it only a decade earlier.

The Outside World Invited In

Bullet Tree Falls was the recipient of two layers of transplanted cultural scenes. The first was militant politics and the ideals of Black power promoted by Hyde and inspired by Garvey. During the latter part of the twentieth century, a second layer produced a quite different cultural scene characterized by themes of unity, harmony, and acceptance of ethnic differences. The music of Bob Marley and the teachings of Henry Coleman transmitted the aura and ideals of Rastafarianism, a kinder, softer Afro-centric culture. Gentrification came after this second layer of a transplanted Rastafarian scene, provided another cultural layer of the village which had become a vacation spot and tropical refuge for an international scene. The end of this flow of related trends was a pattern found elsewhere in the world; a new value on ethnic identify, pride, and countercultural expression opens a culture to the diversity of the world outside.

While Belizean Creoles outside of the village, honored the heritage of Garvey and Hyde and recognized the importance of Marley, they could be quite skeptical of this new craze over the Rasta scene. One time in Belmopan, I met with a noted historian of the Creole political movement to learn more about Rastafarian history in Belize. This gentleman was reluctant to comment on romance tourism, but allowed his younger colleagues to offer their opinions. One of these young men was quick to tell me that they deplored the "rent-a-dread" practice of Rasta men, who are always ready to capitalize on the attentions of female tourists.

It was Rastafarians, certainly not Black power activists inspired by Garvey and Hyde, who were largely responsible for ending a sense of colonial isolation in Bullet Tree Falls, a worldview originally cultivated by the British to reinforce their exclusive right to rule. Instead of presenting a stance in opposition to the rest of the colonizing world, familiarly called the developed "North," they were welcoming. The once closed community provided a hospitable arena for travelers seeking adventure, a place to vacation, a second home, or a retirement refuge. Villagers and visitors alike were seeking a more satisfying lifestyle, and in celebrating cultural diversity, each with economic benefits. Outsiders could buy into the community and had a ready source of labor for land maintenance and domestic tasks; villagers had a new source of employment.

Anthropologist Arjun Appadurai's writings about "scapes" applies here as we see how ideas, habits of thought, and cultural symbols spread around the globe. Appadurai identifies five different categories of scapes: two of these—ideoscapes and mediascapes—are relevant to understanding Creole culture in Belize. In this case, ideoscapes, which consist of ideas contained in highly charged political messaging, arrived first with emphasis on separatism, militancy, class differences, and ethnicity. Next came mediascapes, which consist of cultural images and ideals transmitted through the media to entertain, educate, and change cultural underpinnings, in this case in the person of troubadour Bob Marley who popularized themes of oneness and love central to the Rastafarian faith. Marley's reggae music on the radio, in cassettes, and in dance clubs played a major role. It set the stage for Henry Coleman's person-to-person teachings; and it encouraged transactions that raised the self-esteem and facilitated a positive acceptance of Creole identity in Bullet Tree Falls.

4/The Cooperative Movement

In the 1970s, a new generation of economic planners thought they could create a more prosperous village life by introducing worker-owned/worker-managed cooperatives based on principles of collectivism and cooperation. This new vision of economic advancement in village agriculture began to take hold in 1979, two years before Belize gained independence. It promised to bring Bullet Tree Falls a brighter future (Figure 4.1), just as leaders such as George Price were striving to develop the possibilities of a new nation.[1]

INITIAL AGRICULTURAL COOPERATIVES[2]

The introduction of cooperatives in Bullet Tree Falls presented considerable challenges because villagers would have to learn new attitudes and behavior, leaving behind a tradition of individually laboring on their small plots of land for *milpa* agriculture. However, things did not work out as had been planned. Villagers were proud of their historic occupation as small farmers (*milperos*) and valued the independence and self-reliance that it afforded them. In fact, the farmers in Bullet Tree Falls were especially tenacious in holding onto these farming traditions, far more so than farmers in the neighboring villages of Santa Familia and Succotz. Through door-to-door inquiry, I counted 180 active *milpas* still in existence in Bullet Tree Falls, in contrast to the other two villages where most farmers had sold their land and completely abandoned *milpa* production.

Milperos in Bullet Tree Falls strove for excellence and could identify outstanding farmers whom they admired and respected. I frequently heard villagers use the term "*buen milpero*" (good *milpa* farmer), indicating a revered status. If the farmer was older, in his seventies, then the tone was noticeably reverent, and even more so if he was in his eighties or nineties. Older farmers bragged about never missing a day of work, rising early in the morning at 5:00 A.M., returning home at 11:00 A.M. in the heat of the day, and then putting in a few more hours of work in the afternoon. In actuality, I often saw them walking to work with machetes in hand 7 o'clock in the morning, not around 5:00 A.M., and not all returned to their fields at all in the afternoon. Not uncommonly, they exaggerated their commitment, wanting so much to enhance their claim to individual excellence as farmers.

Women made it possible for men to be so single-minded about their work in the fields. Quite stoically, they got up at the crack of dawn and went about their household chores, without any fuss or boasting—starting fires for the early morning meal, making tortillas, preparing food throughout the day, and taking care of children.

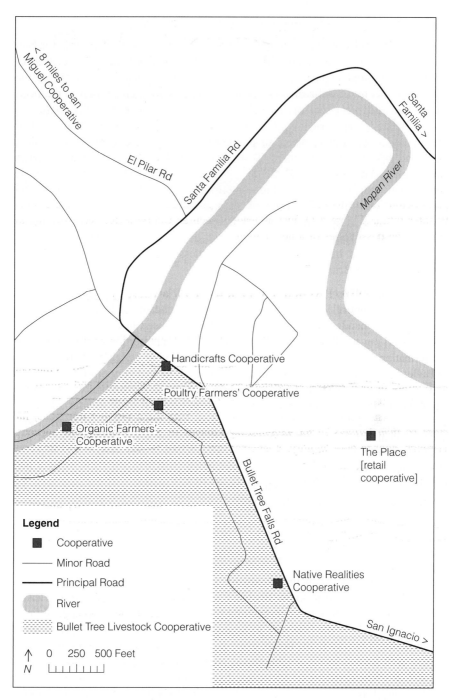

Figure 4.1 Village center—cooperatives.

Assad Shoman and Liberation Theology

The actual task of implementing the plan to establish cooperative farms fell to Assad Shoman, who expressed his intention to use government action to shape a new kind of social equality grounded in collective enterprise. Eleven years before the beginning of the cooperative movement, Shoman returned to Belize in 1968, after studying law and international relations in England. In England and elsewhere during the 1960s a youth movement reached its peak in 1968. Young people were rising up publicly against the "power structure" in demonstrations and riots not just in London, but also in major European capitals and cities and university campuses throughout the United States. In the U.S., bringing the Vietnam War to an end was the primary focus, but demonstrators formed a broad swath of protest, against monopolistic capitalism, imperialism, materialistic society, antiquated sexual mores, and the denial of civil rights.

Shoman brought the "spirit of '68" back to Belize, as he co-founded the Revopolitical Action Movement, which combined the words "revolution" and "political." The party rejected traditional party politics, which he characterized as "a regime of smothering free minds and voices" (McPherson 1995: vii). However, in 1971, Shoman softened his approach and joined Price's People's United Party attempting to use party politics as a means to broaden his influence. Soon thereafter, Price encouraged Shoman to move to Cayo to run for the office of District Representative in the national legislature. In San Ignacio, where Shoman had core support, he raised political consciousness by teaching "weekly liberation classes," held at a location on Bullet Tree Road, a three miles strip extending from San Ignacio to Bullet Tree Falls. His teachings focused on the ills of capitalism, colonialism, racism, and exploitation, while praising the alternative leadership of socialist Prime Minister Michael Manley of Jamaica and communist President Fidel Castro of Cuba.

Shoman's message overlapped with the ideas of Liberation Theology, a Marxist improvisation of Catholicism, proposing that Christianity should be oriented toward class struggle that favored the oppressed, who suffered from exploitation at the hands of the ownership classes. To orient the local population towards the goal of independence, Shoman and others in the San Ignacio area organized what people called "Solidarity Concerts" or "Farmer's Masses" (*Misas Campesinas*), held in open fields on the outskirts of Bullet Tree Falls in the years 1978–81. Carlos Godoy, a singer and spokesman for Liberation Theology among socialist Nicaraguans in the 1970s, came to participate in the meetings and sing inspirational songs that highlighted the spirit of Liberation Theology. Here is a stanza from one of his songs:

> *Christ man, Christ worker [to pursue]*
> *Victory over death ... for liberation ...*
> *To defend the people*
> *Against exploitation*
> *I believe in your ceaseless struggle*
> *I believe in your resurrection.*

With permission of the Canadian Co-operative Association. Photo: John Julian

Figure 4.3 San Miguel Cooperative meeting around 1984.

The Early Phase of Village Cooperatives

In 1979, after he was elected as the Cayo representative to the national legislature, Price appointed Shoman as the Minister of Health, Housing, and Cooperatives. Then Shoman oversaw the establishment of two nationally acclaimed cooperatives in Bullet Tree Falls. One of these was the San Miguel Cooperative (Figure 4.3), which consisted of a fifteen members farming grain on land located eight miles from Bullet Tree Falls next to El Pilar. Each member tended a 50-acre *milpa* plot and shared an additional 200 acres designated for collective cultivation. The other operation was the Bullet Tree Livestock Cooperative, which was set up similar to the San Miguel Cooperative except that the common land was dedicated to grazing a cowherd rather than to the cultivation of grain. Also, individual holdings were smaller, each member taking individual responsibility for only 25 acres of *milpa*. This livestock operation was partially located inside the town limits of Bullet Tree Falls on the same property that had been owned by the Samuels family before land redistribution.

Shoman and other political activists attempted to strengthen the influence of the cooperative movement by sponsoring the First Experimental Laboratory for the Training of Cooperatives, an event held over a three-week period in 1983 on the grounds of the San Miguel cooperative for the benefit of farmers who were members of other cooperatives in the Cayo district. One main purpose of the laboratory was to provide farmers with practical education, which included techniques for constructing irrigation systems, outhouses, and schools, and the use of charcoal for cooking and lime for processing corn. Another main purpose was to raise the spirit and consciousness of farmers, encouraging them to understand their place in the history of the cooperative movement. One Cayo farmer captured the mood by writing a song with lyrics that appeared in the booklet accompanying the event:

> *Farmers all together, we follow the road of our destiny ...*
> *We learn in the seminar, we give thanks.*
> *We feel it in our hearts all that we learned ...*
> *We will go forth, strong, working all together,*
> *We go forth, our hands together every single day.*

Motivated to express their feelings during the training sessions, farmers frequently gave testimony to their commitment to unity and collaboration, and their belief in the importance of God's essential help for achieving success (see San Miguel, 1983).

INCOMPATIBILITIES WITH VILLAGE CULTURE

Despite a promising start and surrounding hoopla, the two cooperatives in Bullet Tree Falls did not run smoothly. Later, during my stay in the village, I heard a litany of complaints from former members about things that went wrong.

Attitudes Toward Government

In principle it seemed that the government had been especially generous in the start-up phase—the initial salaries, the tools, the loans, and so forth. But the scheme went awry when farmers turned around and sold the items that were provided to them, pocketing the money. Farmers even stripped down a donated tractor and sold it piecemeal—the wheels, the radiator, the alternator, and the engine. The system of loans presented problems, as well. In many instances farmers used the loan money to purchase luxury items for their households rather than tools and equipment. Individual members purchased television sets and electrical appliances in anticipation of the day when the town would have its own electrical grid. Even more problematic was the reckless dissipation of a considerable amount of loan money in drinking sprees. The largest flaw in loan program was that farmers simply did not pay back the loans, regardless of whether they had used the money wisely or poorly. The government recognized the problem, but in order not to lose political support in the community, it was not aggressive either about calling in the loans or about seizing land that farmers had used for collateral.

The cynical attitudes toward the government programs on display in Bullet Tree Falls had been shaped historically by oppressive policies and administrative practices that favored large landowners and logging companies over small farmers. Never having received government largesse and being completely unfamiliar with the notion of borrowing and investment, villagers did not know what to make of the loan program. The design of the cooperative program in theory was to empower villagers, but it instead aroused old resentments and suspicions about the motives of government, prompting them to protect what they regarded as their individual interests.

A Culture Shaped by Individual Interests

Among Maya-Mestizos, the older generation of men traditionally set the standards of behavior: individualistic, family-centered, and not given to cooperation even with brothers. A strong preference for individual work was always the norm in Bullet Tree Falls. A good example is my friend Albert Manolo, who owned a *milpa* farm adjacent to the farms of his three brothers. Each of the brothers cultivated seven acres inherited from their father several decades earlier. Harboring no jealousy or rancor over the value of their land holdings or relative wealth, the brothers socialized frequently, always ready to greet one another and talk, but they never helped each other when it came to farming.

I remarked to Albert that surely they would benefit from reciprocity, pitching in and assisting on labor-intensive tasks that must be done quickly, such as clearing land and harvesting. I suggested that they might work together as a group on such specific tasks. Albert assured me that they always worked alone, finding any necessary assistance from their sons, not their brothers. If a son was not available, they hired a laborer from outside the family to do the work. Brothers were cautious in their interactions, sometimes feeling and acting estranged from each other, especially avoiding the issue of inheritance. Accusations of cozying up to a father in his later years to gain ownership of a bigger portion of family land were easily provoked. As well, work proffered to a brother might not be returned, creating difficulties that could last. Best to avoid the whole matter of reciprocity.

Family ties were not always absent. Family members were to be found in the same cooperatives and there was a degree of cooperation, however, it was only brief. The national Department of Cooperatives approved a cooperative only when there were at least ten applicants. Kin approached each other to sign up as members. But the strength of kin ties stopped there. After the membership number was reached and the cooperative became official, each individual pursued his own interests.

Individual cooperative members who might go to great lengths to gain a family advantage still hesitated to exercise any initiative on behalf of the entire membership, as illustrated by an incident that occurred in 1983 in the Bullet Tree Livestock Cooperative. Suddenly and quite mysteriously a cow dropped dead. Veterinarians from the Department of Agriculture came out to investigate, and found that the cow had fallen victim to a highly contagious worm infestation, likely to spread to other cows and kill off the whole herd. The veterinarians were ready to inoculate the remaining cows as soon as one member of the cooperative signed a note regarding the cooperative's intention to cover the cost of the inoculations. No member wanted to sign the agreement, or even cared that much about the inoculations or the fate of the herd. Finally to save the herd, the veterinarians just stepped in and did the work without the payment agreement.

Later that same year, four members of the Livestock Cooperative resigned, claiming they had lost confidence, and described the management as "rotten." Among the remaining nine members, no one wanted to associate with anyone else. In 1984, the president of the Livestock Cooperative assessed the situation as unsalvageable and dissolved the membership.

Irregular Benefits, Irregular Patterns of Work

Based on bitter experience, members of the San Miguel Cooperative had no faith that marketing their crops would bring them a steady income. In 1982, they lost an entire season's harvest due to the incompetence of the government's marketing director, who knew little about agriculture and less about marketing, urging them to plant as much corn as possible to meet his unrealistic projections of a growth in demand. Instead the farmers faced a worldwide glut of corn production that year. With nowhere to sell their harvest, they could do nothing but watch the corn rot in their fields.

In the early years of the San Miguel Cooperative, villagers were making a transition from an economy largely based on subsistence farming to a money-driven society, in which they always needed cash to pay their bills for water and electricity, store-bought clothes, and their children's schooling. To make ends meet in an uncertain market economy, some members of the cooperative periodically travelled around the county to find temporary jobs, usually in construction or tourism. While they were away, their cousins or other relatives sometimes filled in, but they were even less committed to the cooperative than the members themselves. Among the cooperative members, there were some diligent members who came to work every day yet their indifference toward the cooperative grew as they complained about the unreliable participation of some colleagues, remarking that absences from work lasted for weeks at a time.

At times, the atmosphere at the San Miguel Cooperative was more like that of a leisure zone than a worksite. After years of hard work, they saw the cooperative as an opportunity to relax and enjoy themselves after having labored so hard as independent small farmers. They saw the cooperative as a chance to take it easy for an extended period magnifying what was, otherwise an abbreviated spell of leisure. In the past after selling their crops in the market in San Ignacio, they often headed for the bars where they took "time out," a temporary escape from responsibility described in Craig MacAndrew and Robert B. Edgerton's book *Drunken Comportment: A Social Explanation* (1969). When the cooperative began, workers frequently took "time out" well before a harvest to the detriment of their collective crop, which suffered from neglect. The cooperative became a place to drink, substituting for a bar; for some it was also a haven for smoking marijuana. Hector, who gave up teaching for a couple of years to try his luck working for the cooperative, told me that although some members smoked and worked hard, many others smoked, went to sleep, got up to eat, smoked once more, and then went back to sleep. We laughed!

Don Capo believed that he led the "good life" as a member of the cooperative. He would leave home on his horse early Monday morning at dawn, well provisioned for five days with easy-to-carry items, such as tortillas and beans. Two and a half hours later he would arrive at the cooperative to work until Friday, after which he and his horse would return home. He regarded his life at the cooperative as a "luxury," and with a confident smile described how members had access to fertile land, a creek for bathing, and a more comfortable climate at a higher altitude where he could enjoy taking long walks.

Distrust of Leaders

Leaders of cooperatives had difficulty finding support and exercising authority because Bullet Tree Falls had no tradition of being governed by formal leaders, except for the village mayor (*alcalde*) whose major responsibilities were organizing community clean-ups (*faenas*) and keeping the peace during village-wide social events, which mostly involved locking up unruly drunks in a stockade. Also contributing to distrust were unfavorable experiences with authorities, especially those sent into the community by colonial administrators as well as private contractors to supervise villagers in the work of collecting tree resin (called *chicle*), the essential ingredient used in manufacturing chewing gum, in this case sold under the brand of Beechnut Gum. Knowing that in the past colonial authorities and contractors had been inconsiderate and exploitative, villagers anticipated the same treatment from any leader, including one they had elected as head of their own cooperative.

Cooperative members were sincere in trying to find the best person to serve in a role of authority as their president, but the qualities that made someone electable were the same qualities that made him untrustworthy—being literate, articulate, good with numbers, and comfortable in meetings with government authorities. These otherwise desirable qualities were suspect because such a leader would have the skills and connections to embezzle funds and cheat other members, perhaps by skimming off a percentage from the purchase of supplies and sale of crops. Villagers facetiously described leaders of cooperatives as *listo*, meaning "ready," implying that they were ready to make off with land, livestock, machinery, and any other valuable items they might get their hands on. Villagers even accused some leaders of deliberately ruining the cooperative in order to dissolve it and keep the remaining assets for themselves. They often described leaders as "lizards" and "bandits."

Don Tomas, the first elected president of San Miguel Cooperative, began his term with a considerable amount of respect. He was literate, savvy, and enthusiastic about the possibilities of developing a modern, mechanized cooperative. As one who always kept up with the latest technological and organizational advances, he became a star in a wider circle of experts recognized to be authorities on successful management of cooperatives. However, his travels around the Caribbean Basin to participate in meetings and training sessions raised suspicions among members of the San Miguel Cooperative that their funds were going to support unwarranted personal travel. The result was that in the next election members threw him out of office.

CANADA REVIVES THE COOPERATIVE IDEAL

In 1985, the Canadian government intervened to play a major role cultivating what were to have been socialist-style cooperatives in Belize. As told to me personally by George Price, he and Pierre Elliot Trudeau, a popular Prime Minister of Canada in the 1970s, became good friends during Trudeau's fishing trip to Belize in 1971, and afterwards kept in touch on a regular basis. Price commented:

> We were good friends, and he tried to help us, he did his best ... to help Belize; in fact, some people in Canada were criticizing him for too much friendship.

Trudeau and Price were both regarded as "fathers" of their respective countries, setting a course that conferred dignity and citizenship rights on everyone. Trudeau restored the rights of the indigenous peoples of Canada, the so-called "First Nations," and made material restitution for past depredations. Price restored land and dignity to the Maya-Mestizo people.

Both Trudeau and Price were guided as humanitarians by the ethic of Catholic social justice. For a period of time in his life, Trudeau attended daily mass, as Price had done throughout his life. Several commonalities linked the two countries and their two presidents—both were part of the British Commonwealth, both were English-speaking, and both understood the key role of independence as part of nationhood, having decolonized from England. This natural affinity between the two countries resulted in Canada providing substantial development aid to Belize. In the 1970s and 1980s, the Canadian government financed a water and sewage development project for Belize City, costing CA $35 million, and in 1982, funded the construction of agricultural silos throughout the country. Most importantly, for our interests, from 1985 through 1994 Canada played a formative role in funding and supporting the cooperative movement.[3]

The Canadian Cooperative Tradition

Canada's commitment to the cooperative movement began in the early part of the twentieth century, and subsequently became intertwined with Canada's political culture, shaped by social democrats, and characterized by the dominance of what was known as the "Third Force," consisting of a moderate social and political agenda—neither extremely conservative nor extremely liberal—neither entirely capitalist nor entirely socialist.

In her 1986 book, *More Than Just a Job: Worker Cooperatives in Canada*, journalist Constance Mungall reported that 43 percent of all Canadians over the age of 18 were members of at least one cooperative, one million of them belonging to retail cooperatives. She also found that cooperative farms marketed 80 percent of Canada's dairy products. Another report revealed that in the 1980s, cooperatives accounted for 70 percent of Canada's national grain production, 34 percent of its poultry output, and 30 percent of its feed and fertilizer industry.[4]

During the 1980s, cooperatives became a central subject in Canadian education, as universities across Canada began offering programs in cooperatives studies. For example, in western Canada's prairie states, the University of Saskatchewan established the Center for the Study of Co-operatives in 1984; and several years later, the Universities of Alberta in British Columbia, and the University of Manitoba followed suit to fund faculty positions or institutes specializing in cooperative studies.

Father Coady's Inspiration

The Catholic university of St. Francis Xavier in Antigonish, Nova Scotia, began a program of education and outreach to establish cooperatives in 1928, in response to severe poverty and economic stagnation in rural Nova Scotia. According to a news article about the development of the Coady Center, Father Moses Coady, a professor at St. Xavier University, had witnessed the poverty firsthand, describing what he saw: "Nova Scotia wallowed in the depressive 1920s, with fishing boats rotting on the beaches, and farmers eating their badly-needed livestock."[5] Coady, promoted the development of workers' cooperatives, buyers' cooperatives, and credit unions throughout Nova Scotia. Success inspired him to propose a plan for expanding his cooperative program to underdeveloped areas around the world. Though implementation was delayed for financial reasons, in 1961, two years after Coady's death, St. Francis Xavier established the Coady Institute based on his philosophy of adult education to promote the global spread of cooperative through local initiatives. For half a century, the Coady Institute has worked in more than 150 countries worldwide, including Belize.

Coady, like Price, was focused on social justice as inspired by papal encyclicals. In a 1956 article in *The Canadian Register*, a Catholic publication, Coady highlights the most important features of the social justice movement envisioned by the Vatican. He cites a passage from Pope Pius XI's *Quadragesimo Anno*, written to celebrate the 40-year anniversary of the writing of the *Rerum Novarum* by Pope Leo XIII:

> Immense power and despotic economic domination is concentrated in the hands of a few. This power becomes irresistible when exercised by those who, because they hold and control money, are able to govern credit and determine its allotment.... Free competition is dead; economic dictatorship takes its place.... The whole economic life has become hard, cruel and relentless in a ghostly measure (see Laidlaw 1971: 128).[6]

Like Price who travelled by Land Rover, and sometimes by mule, to all parts of Belize, Coady stayed close to "the people" by driving his Buick to the far corners of Nova Scotia and the Maritime Provinces. When roads were covered with snow, he drove a horse and sleigh. Coady organized study clubs so that farmers could learn about the political philosophy, expected benefits, administrative practices, and the organization of production in cooperative enterprises. In his own words, Coady's priorities were to promote education about cooperatives and sustain cooperative ventures and credit unions in a mixed economic system, which included both individual and collective ownership, leaving room for both private profit and collective benefit.

Coady never visited Belize, though his teachings and philosophy were transmitted by his staff to several generations of Belizeans, including both managers and workers who were involved first with credit unions and fishing cooperatives and later with agricultural cooperatives. From 1963 to 1979, the Coady Institute received funding support from the Canadian government to bring 43 Belizean leaders in administration of governmental and non-profit entities to the Coady Institute in Nova Scotia where they often engaged in six months of intensive study in the development, management, and political philosophy of cooperatives. Then from 1984 to 1988, Coady Institute trainers regularly travelled to Belize to provide the same kind of training on agricultural cooperatives, altogether conducting 127 weekend sessions attended by 3,277 Belizeans.

Canada's Prime Minister Mulroney and his Impact on
Cooperatives, Starting in 1984

The Canadian Co-operative Association (CCA), founded in 1909, acted as a clearinghouse to share information and bring together representatives of domestic and international cooperative organizations. The CCA always maintained strong ties with the Coady Institute and together they sought to change the way work and workers were organized in Belize. In 1983, the head of the Department of Cooperatives in Belize, a graduate of the leadership program at the Coady Institute, requested that the CCA send an expert to Belize to assess its potential for expanding its cooperative movement. Steven Adler, a recent Ph.D. graduate of the University of Wisconsin who had a special interest in Latin America, accepted this assignment. Smart and impulsive, Adler found himself inspired while waiting at a bus station in Belize City; he noticed that bus arrival and departure times were displayed on the walls in paint, rather than in pencil. He inferred from this observation that Belizeans were really committed to a certain schedule and an organized way of doing things, not constantly improvising, a dysfunctional trait he had encountered while working in Colombia a few years earlier. Thus, he believed that people in Belize would be true to their word, or so it seemed. At that time, the CCA mandate was, in the words of one of their program presentations, to work in a "favorable environment for co-operative development," and Adler judged the environment in Belize to be favorable.[7]

In 1985, the CCA made a commitment to give regular funding support to cooperatives in Belize and establish an office with in-country support staff. Adler characterized his team of workers as:

> Shaped by the cutting-edge thinking on development of that time—Paolo Freire's *Pedagogy of the Oppressed*, Monsgr. Ivan Illich's *Deschooling Society*, Julius K. Nyerere's the *Arusha Declaration*. We were focused on development from the bottom up in a time of new nations and high hopes.

Twenty five years later in 2011 during a visit to the Canadian Co-operative Association Office in Ottawa, I found that the same kind of idealistic spirit prevailed, both among young workers dressed very casually and among older ones who looked like summer-stock versions of old hippies. In Belize local managers in the cooperative movement were infected by the same utopian drive as the Canadians, which came as a result of their interactions with members of the political party of George Price, the training they received from the Coady Institute staff, and their communications with the idealistic staff at the CCA office.

Cooperatives for Capitalists

But, the rules changed in the year 1984, when Brian Mulroney, leader of the Progressive Conservative Party, replaced Trudeau as Prime Minister of Canada. The change in government was part of a conservative trend that swept through the politics of Canada, Great Britain, and the United States in the 1980s. The set-up looked cooperativist but really the model of behavior was capitalist and competitive.

In line with the policies of Margaret Thatcher, British Prime Minister from 1979–1990, and Ronald Reagan, U.S. President from 1980 to 1988, Mulroney opposed what he called "give away" policies typical of the previous Trudeau government, and pursued a policy of "assertive globalism," which meant developing private sector business opportunities abroad and expanding Canada's international commercial ties.[8]

Starting in 1985 the Canadian government provided 12 million Canadian dollars every three years to the CCA which used the funds for use its own staff and reallocated the majority of the money abroad, sending the money to the CCA which used some of the funds for its own staff while the CCA allocated the rest of the money to foreign in-country supervisory organizations – "apex organizations" – whose job was to support to varied cooperatives in that foreign country. The strategy was intended to outsource the national government's work and to transfer the responsibilities to private sources, the CCA and the apex organizations (mostly NGOs) that were programmed to facilitate purchases of equipment, to provide technical assistance and to make money available for loans.[9] This 12 million dollar budget to the CCA went to about twenty countries in the developing world. The funding of the CCA was a manifestation of Mulroney's willingness to support private organizations, moving away from reliance on government to do all the work. Previously, during the Trudeau years the governmental Canadian International Development Association had the major responsibility for many international development initiatives. But, in the mid-1980s, the Canadian Co-operative Association took over the work with cooperatives. Government work was outsourced to this organization, a private NGO, and the size of the CCA staff went from 7 to 28 people.

The favored status of the private sector in Canada matched what was going on in Belize. In 1984, George Price was voted out of office and a new Belizean government was to be led by Prime Minister Manuel Esquivel. His United Democratic Party had trounced George Price and his party in the election of 1984. Many Belizeans began to think Price was behind a plan for one-party rule in a communist political system, as evidenced by his friendship with Fidel Castro and his commandeering vision of Belize's future. A majority had decisively voted for Manuel Esquivel because of his commitment to a strong and unfettered private sector.

The new recruits to the NGOs in Belize and the new recruits in the CCA were a similar sort—idealistic, optimistic, and full of imagination. In both cases many of them had left government jobs, and were pleased to be free of government rules and procedures, thus allowing them to apply their skills in a self-directed and creative manner. What NGO staff members in Belize did not realize was the degree to which they had traded off the security of a steady government job for a new set of pressures working in a competitive marketplace; with one NGO competing against another. The three NGOs were in stiff competition with each other for contracts to manage new projects proposed by international donors. Their very existence was continuously threatened, and the jobs of their employees were at risk. Finding themselves chronically short of money and staff, they had to divert much of their effort to getting new contracts, often with insufficient time to spend on their primary mission of developing cooperatives.

The Esquivel government was wholly supportive of the NGOs, and the private sector generally. In one case, the Belizean national government went so far as to allow one NGO to into go into business for itself by importing food from Mexico to be sold in Belize.

Generally, the government style was not to regulate or to look closely at what the NGOs were doing. One of the Belmopan based NGOs established and managed a retail cooperative in Bullet Tree Falls which was called "The Place." At The Place, villagers could buy items for everyday needs such as flour, soap, sugar, salt, and so forth. It turned out that the cooperative's source to buy these supplies was not chosen as a result of a conscientious search for the cheapest products. Instead, there was just one main supplier for the cooperative and the supplies to be provided by the mother of a government official. Clearly this was some sort of political payback. Generally, the experience of working in The Place had little resemblance to the way a cooperative should work. The cooperative's treasurer never saw a bank statement, and the members were wholly uninformed about its operations and finances. Essentially, they were treated as if they were employees, not equal partners. The cooperative members soon began to suspect that supplier was making unreasonable profits. Members became dispirited and cynical about the whole operation. They habitually "borrowed" food and household utensils from the shelves, and helped themselves to a portion of the money while working at the cash register. After six years, the store shelves were empty, no money was left in reserve, no one wanted to work there anymore, and, according to rumor, an arsonist burned the building to the ground, to deflect attention from theft (Figure 4.4).

Reprise in Bullet Tree Falls

In 1985, San Miguel had replaced the unpopular Don Tomas in the role of president of the cooperative with Don Capo as president. At the time, Don Capo was intent on reviving the vision of Price and Shoman, apparently yet more possible because of the infusion of Canadian money. He delivered eloquent speeches to workers. Don Beto described Don Capo as a "troubadour" who sang the praise of cooperatives. Don Capo's outward enthusiasm, however, was soon followed by the disappointment he expressed in a written memorandum to the Department of Agriculture calling attention to major problems: 1) a lack of cooperative spirit, 2) the use of the storage facility to store marijuana, 3) thefts of tools, and 4) selling collective crops individually. At the same time cooperative members became disillusioned with Don Capo, and he too became the subject of rumors about the disappearing tools and equipment. The grand plans of the cooperatives finally went up in flames, quite literally, as the cooperative storage building burned (once again this happens) to the ground in a suspected arson seemingly motivated by a desire to burn evidence that linked cooperative members to the thefts of tools and equipment. At the end of the year the members of the cooperative voted out Don Capo as president.

During the same year, one of the NGOs operating out of Belmopan tried to revive the Bullet Tree Livestock Cooperative, this time to sell grains and peanuts on the international market instead of raising cows. However, its members seemed

Figure 4.4 Remains of The Place (the retail cooperative) after arson finished it off.

less interested in farming than in obtaining personal loans that were a privilege of cooperative membership. The amount they all borrowed was staggering—a sum of BZ $227,000—none of it repaid to the lenders, which included loans from the CCA, a Belizean government reserve bank, and a local private bank, the latter being the only one to recoup some of its losses by repossessing land.

The problem went deeper than failing to meet repayment obligations; members demonstrated a fundamental lack of interest in the cooperative. From 1987 to 1989, when the cooperative was supposed to have come back to life, it held no meetings. In reviewing documents in the archives of the Department of Cooperatives, I found that members had warned the government that its president was planning to skip out of the country with BZ $10,000 belonging to the cooperative. The government did nothing, and the president left with money to start a new life in the United States. By 1990, the cooperative had fully disbanded.

In 1994, the Canadian Co-operative Association completely halted its work in Belize, claiming that it could not attract a sufficient number of participant organizations under the supervision of its NGOs to make their efforts worthwhile. The experience of trying to set up cooperatives was a regrettable tale of idealism, energy, and commitment subverted by the individual self-interest of participants, the remoteness of the NGO superstructure, a lack of financial controls and the absence of individual responsibility throughout the system. Investments by the Canadians amounted to an expensive exercise in futility, as recipients never managed to put into practice any cooperative ideals. Though no doubt well meaning, the Canadians had no clear idea of the problems involved in the merging of interests and ideologies of the private sector and cooperatives, much less how to solve them. Following these efforts the cooperative movement in the village was relatively quiet from 1994 to 2008, during which time the El Pilar Project grasped people's attention.

DONORS FOCUSED ON TECHNOCRATIC DEVELOPMENT

Another phase of the cooperative movement began in 2008, 14 years after the CCA had packed up and gone home, this time sponsored by a different set of international donors—the European Union, the Agroforestry Foundation, and the Canadian Fund for Local Initiatives, the latter being a small program administered by the Canadian Embassy representative for Belize. The emphasis in this phase was on building technical capacity in the rural sector, still bringing people together in the context of a larger enterprise, but with less concern for promoting cooperative ideals. The program found its operating principles in the free market doctrine of the famous English philosopher, Adam Smith, and other theoreticians of capitalism. Major international institutions that commonly set the agenda for other donors, such as the Food and Agriculture Organization, the United Nations, and the World Bank, viewed cooperatives as an optimal framework for bringing people together to transfer technology and knowledge, as opposed to the transfer of technology and knowledge proceeding in a much less controlled and irregular fashion from one individual to another. Basically, major international donors expected that cooperatives would lay the groundwork for prosperity, and that the inevitable forces of capitalism would do the rest, whereby markets would spontaneously emerge from the trainees' increased technical capacity.

In this last phase, my research strategy was different in that I could see what was going on, not just listening to people's recollections of what happened two or three decades ago. I offer the reader some of what I saw and heard firsthand.

The Native Realities Cooperative

The European Union that financed the Belize Rural Development Program staked out a new jewelry and sculpture cooperative, called the Native Realities Cooperative, with financing of BZ $25,000 in 2008. To get the story, I spoke with the president of the cooperative, Luisa, who was 38 years old, married, with several children. Making crafts was her passion. Starting early in the morning with an idea for a new design, she would get right to work on the product. While I spoke with her, we sat in the single room of her workshop, located inside a newly constructed, bright-blue, 20×16-foot house. The surroundings consisted of workbenches with machine tools for cutting, sanding, and shaping, as well as vices, knives, wires, and pincers. Finished products on display and ready for sale included necklaces, bracelets, and images of sharks fashioned out of cow horn. She told me that members were enthusiastic in the beginning and excited about learning new skills and making extra money. The cooperative represented a chance for wives to make a substantial contribution to household income and family prosperity.

I emphasized to Luisa that I was interested in learning about the problems of artisan cooperatives. Her response identified many of the same issues that had existed 30 years earlier with the first two agricultural cooperatives in Bullet Tree

Falls. Two obvious differences between the cooperatives of the past and Luisa's cooperative were that hers was composed only of women, and they were doing artisan work, not agriculture. Regardless of these differences and the lapse of 30 years the problems were the same—distrust of leadership, members going off in their own direction, profitability not being apparent to members, low morale, and lack of participation. Luisa commented on her frustrations:

> For me the difficult thing is that this is the first time that ... I am a chairperson and I don't know what to discuss with the group. The members don't help you, you know, and they say I have to do my agenda for each meeting, and I really can't do it. They want to have a record of the agenda every meeting. To run a group you have to know a lot. I have to know a lot and I've never been with another group. And you can't do anything with just four or five members; the rest don't show up, ever.

Although an occasional sale was gratifying, the attitude quickly turned to resentment when members had to turn back 40 percent of their sales to the cooperative to buy new tools, repair broken ones, replenish supplies such as wire and glue, and pay the electricity bills. Necessary trips around the country to market their wares were expensive. Luisa reported that on one trip she spent BZ $40 for taxi fares compared to product sales of BZ $80. Another 40 percent, or BZ $16, went back into the cooperative, leaving BZ $24 to be divided among five individual members, amounting to less than five dollars each. It wasn't worth the trouble.

According to the rules of the cooperative, the members were supposed to work only three days per week to allow them time for other activities, but it did not take long before they stopped coming completely. Luisa lamented her plight:

> They take advantage of me, wanting me to go out and develop places to sell. We started as a group, but there is no group right now. People don't show ... And I don't know what I could do and it's confusing me now. I can come half a day, afterwards I have to clean my house. I want to have a group meeting to discuss how we could go forward and sell. But it's not possible. Last time we had a meeting was 15 March 2010 [15 months previously].

The lack of visitors to the anemic tourism venture at El Pilar ended any hope of a local market. It all seemed to be a bust. Luisa had the support of her husband and family to ditch the effort, but she never quite let go, at least during my time in the village. One clearly positive note is that the workshop did not become a target for theft, and soon Luisa transformed it into a center for the use of several of her family members.

The Handicrafts Cooperative

The Handicrafts Cooperative began in 2008, with funds from the World Bank and other major donors funneled through the Agroforestry Foundation then going to the cooperative. Membership consisted of ten women who expressed enthusiasm about creating a better future for themselves and their families. Initially, various trainers taught them how to work with clay, use the pottery wheel, bake ceramics, and run the sewing machines. Their enthusiasm began to wane when no sales were forth-coming. The cooperative faced problems similar to those of the Native Realities Cooperative—lack of motivation related to lack of a market for their products. With no income to show for their work, the members wanted to receive an hourly rate, not a commission based on sales. Finding this scenario to be impossible, six disillusioned members dropped out, leaving only four: Imelda, the president of the cooperative, along with her mother, her sister, and her niece. They casually gathered several days per week on the porch of the Cultural Center to make clay cups and bowls, and cute animal figurines for largely their own amusement and minimal sales. This last rem-nant of participants, all family members, seemed to enjoy the companionship, which, ten years earlier would have been shared while sitting by the river to wash clothes.

The Organic Crops Cooperative

In 2008, 15 farmers who were still members of the original Amigos de El Pilar group, now called "Farmers of El Pilar," received a grant from the Canadian Fund for Local Initiatives to cultivate organic crops for sale to restaurants and hotels whose tourist clientele would appreciate locally grown, organic food. A report by an investigator in the Department of Agriculture certified that the plants he exam-ined in the cooperative garden were growing according to international organic standards. The problem was that the cooperative part of the project existed on less than one acre, and the supervisor for the Canadian Fund overlooked the fact that this seemingly model garden was cultivated mostly by just one person, the presi-dent of the Cooperative. It was far cry from a true collective project.

Of the 15 members in the *Amigos* group, 11 expressed initial interest in the organic farming project, but only five actually joined. Among those five, only two, aside from Don Capo, showed up to work with any regularity, and these two were far from being diligent workers. Doña Maria, who spent most of her time selling prepared fast food on the streets of San Ignacio, briefly came by to check on the project once a week. Oscar, Capo's brother, also came by once a week. Like Luisa and Imelda, Don Capo wound up pretty much alone working in the coopera-tive. But for him, the story was different because he had something to sell—organic cabbages, and plenty of them—at a good price, high enough that he could expect to receive BZ $1,500 for the sale of his harvest (Figure 4.5).

THE CULTURE OF DEVELOPMENT WORKERS, GLOBALLY

While conducting fieldwork, I became aware of a culture shared by development workers that precluded critical self-examination of their role as agents of change. While I draw on examples from different phases of the cooperative movement, the illustrations pertain to all its phases, the one initiated by the People's United Party, and the second phase where the Canadian Co-operative Association had so much influence, and the final and third phase with donors focused on technocratic development.

Figure 4.5 Don Capo in his organic garden.

Faulty Assumptions and Public Relations

I questioned why the European Union (EU) staff failed to notice the absence of tourists when they made the decision to fund the Native Realities Cooperative as part of the Belize Rural Development Program. They pointed out to me that they had made efforts to solve the marketing problem, for example, providing free stall space for the Native Realities Cooperative on Saturday mornings at the market in San Ignacio. This market, however, catered to local shoppers who were disinclined to buy tourist souvenirs such as Maya-style jewelry and sculpture. The EU staff made other attempts to help the cooperative, for example, accompanying Luisa to give her advice as she made purchases of jewelry and sculpture materials in supply shops. However, this had no bearing on the real problem of finding a market. The EU staff dismissed their responsibility by attributing the marketing problem to Luisa's personal inability to make management decisions and act authoritatively. According to the prevailing development theory of free markets, technical training offered to cooperative members should have been sufficient for success because competitive human instinct would take over, ensuring that marketing and profit making would naturally emerge.

The reason for the indifference of EU staff to the problems of cooperatives was also related to donor objectives and expectations. The European Union funded small and large projects in various parts of Belize—46 projects in all from 2006 to 2011. Outside each project workshop, clearly visible from the highway, stood the same four-by-three-foot artistic and eye-catching sign highlighting the words "European Union Project" to advertise the donor, followed by the name of the particular cooperative (Figure 4.6). Similarly, the Agroforestry Foundation seemed unconcerned about the fate of the Handicrafts Cooperative, neither scheduling any project evaluations, nor offering any supervision of cooperative operations. Apparently, fulfilling its mandate to provide funding seemed to be enough to satisfy the

Figure 4.6 Sign from the European Community program for cooperatives outside the Native Realities Cooperative.

bureaucracy. Likewise, the Canadian Fund for Local Initiatives, while funding organic farming and reforestation, was heavily committed to self-promotion. One of its high-level development officers in Ottawa candidly informed me that the objective of providing aid to cooperatives was to "spread around the maple leaf" (Canada's iconic national symbol) and get the word out about Canada's goodwill toward developing countries. No matter the successful or unsuccessful outcome of their projects, the donor at all phases would still receive favorable recognition for having spread around its largesse.

Persistent Optimism and Faith

Local change agents working in NGOs seemed to lack awareness of any shortcomings in their approach. Faith in their policies and practices derived from the ideals and teachings of Father Coady and the People's United Party was not subject to empirical challenge. By organizing cooperatives as an act of faith rather than an act of applying practical expertise, they fell short of realizing that they were conducting a risky experiment with the lives and livelihoods of human beings, perhaps with a different life experience and contrasting ideals. They remained persistently optimistic, undeterred from their agenda even when there was so much contradictory evidence.

Political leaders were long on ideology and theory but short on practice. Shoman, appointed to his job by Price, was an intellectual and theoretician, one who likely looked to Cuban farming cooperatives as a model. Cuba's cooperative system, however, had no marketing problem, since it was based on single-crop cultivation with a guaranteed buyer in the Soviet Union. In addition, the values inherent in cooperatives were woven through every level of Cuban society—with Fidel Castro at the top exhorting all workers to develop a new Cuban socialist ethic, a new "Cuban Man." As it turned out, the Cuban experience could not be grafted onto Bullet Tree Falls, despite all the excitement generated by solidarity concerts and the example of Nicaragua.

Recognition of Outcomes, Followed by Inaction

I heard some very hard-nosed, cold assessments of the progress of the cooperative movement, not just in Bullet Tree Falls, but in government offices as well. One official to offer a tale of woe was Don Marco, the Acting Director of the Department of the Cooperatives in Belize. Over lunch one day he gave me his opinion about the Bullet Tree Falls cooperatives, flatly asserting that villagers were incapable of running a decent cooperative, and that the members of the San Miguel Cooperative never had any intention of running a cooperative, just using it as a cover to gain access to land, equipment, and loans for their own individual purposes. His criticism went beyond Bullet Tree Falls, as he regarded all villagers in Belize who signed up as members of cooperatives as *bandidos*—selfish, thieving, irresponsible, and by nature uncooperative and lazy.

Marco even recited a damning statistic: "Of the 215 cooperatives [currently registered] in the country, only 15 are operational." Nevertheless, Marco planned to continue to work in the cooperative movement, and ironically seemed genuinely enthusiastic about the possibilities for ultimate success. In our last conversation in 2012, he told me how cooperatives would soon be making progress. Excitedly, he pointed to new management procedures he put in place to make administration more effective. He seemed content that changes in the way office work was carried out were going to make a difference, but he overlooked the difficulties of administrative staff actually spending time in the cooperatives to identify and solve problems.

Joe Lisbey, another veteran of the cooperative movement for almost three decades, began his career by working in the Belizean Department of Agriculture and then went on to work in an NGO bankrolled largely by Canada. He also stubbornly remained optimistic about the movement, even though evidence that he personally collected suggested that success was elusive and in the end unlikely. In 2007, when the Food and Agriculture Organization (FAO) of the United Nations hired him to review the record of success on farming cooperatives in Belize, he reported disappointing results:

> Of the 135 agricultural cooperatives registered in the country, 40% (53) are in the process of being liquidated or have been dissolved. The balance of the 82 societies is either dormant or semi-active and working, 10% of those agricultural cooperatives are actually active and working (Lisbey 2008: 3–4).

Joe and other administrators like him did not take such statistics seriously perhaps because they did not fully appreciate the roots of failure. Their attitude was that failure was just something that happened, and it was not their fault; but nor was it something for which anyone held them accountable.

The Nature of Not Understanding

The Belizean agents of change in the cooperative movement stayed in their professional comfort zone, interacting with the cooperatives in a way that confirmed their own professional biases. Staff trained in agriculture spent their time with workers discussing issues such as seeds and grasses, not the problems between leaders and followers. Their time spent in the field giving technical advice did not include any efforts to intervene in person-to-person problems. As one NGO agricultural specialist reported:

> I was a technical person [in agriculture]. I was never trained in cooperatives; [it] is more than backbreaking work. I was trained in technical matters and would have been more effective were I to have known the managerial end. In the last ten years my administrative work has not been in farming but in refugee services.... Now I can assess emotions, offer individual help, and solve their problems.

NGO managers charged with addressing issues of leadership and marketing spent their time exclusively with leaders of cooperatives, and they avoided associating with ordinary members who might have been more inclined to disclose problems that needed attention.

Evaluations are a necessary part of any development program, ideally pointing the way to make corrections and avoid debilitating mistakes. In the case of Belizean cooperatives, however, the process of evaluation seems to have been carried out with the purpose of deflecting criticism rather than candidly identifying problems. In the 1980s, Coady trainers in Belize conducted evaluations immediately following their training sessions in Belize City. I asked Eric Amit, who had been one of the principal organizers of the training, about the methods they had used for the evaluation. He recalled that trainees had completed paper and pencil evaluations after each of the training sessions. Asking for feedback on the spot tends to encourage responses far more favorable to the trainers than evaluations done later with complete anonymity for the trainees.

A reliable assessment of training would require actually going to the cooperative and "hanging out" (more formally recognized as the method of "participant observation"), but this method was not part of Coady administrators' routine. Furthermore, the design of the training omitted paying any attention to the distinctive interpersonal and cultural challenges that might present themselves in a Belizean village. In reflecting on Coady's disappointment in being unable to apply the lessons of his successes in Nova Scotia to the French sectors of Maritime Canada, his biographer Jim Lotz reported in his book *The Humble Giant: Moses Coady, Canada's Rural Revolutionary:*

> Father Coady was unaware of the way culture influences outcome; unaware of the need for alternative approaches to encourage people to cooperate. For Coady culture was all about opera and classical music, not about the unique way in which people lived, worked and thought (2005: 118).

The Canadian Co-operative Association apparently borrowed a page from Coady's playbook. Idealistic plans became subverted by unanticipated cultural realities, which they had not investigated. One of the association's staff members in Belize explained how they made only brief "site visits," lasting for a couple of hours, in the context of a prearranged, structured occasion that brought members of the cooperative together in a meeting to engage in discussions. The objective of the site visitor was to assess what evaluators call the "organization's climate," which consisted of attendance, participation, and attitudes expressed in the group meeting. The site visit routine brought back memories of my elementary school where teachers admonished us to be on our best behavior to give a good impression to a distinguished visitor.

The newsletters and reports I observed in the offices of the Canadian Co-operative Association contained only big headlines and stories about successes. Bad news about how cooperatives actually functioned rarely worked its way back to the Canadian Co-operative Association office unless one of its cooperatives was in dire straits and about to collapse. At this late stage, even if CCA authorities had detected problems, they probably would have been unable to offer much help. They recognized their own limited capacity to deal with "the size and number of requests" for assistance, as the number of cooperatives had far outstripped the staff's "ability to respond."[10] With respect to the revival of the cooperative movement in 2008, evaluations were not even part of the program design.

LOCALLY GENERATED SUCCESS

No matter what the plan, coming from collectivist, capitalist, technocratic, or any other theoretical underpinning, the vast majority of cooperatives in Belize did not measure up to expectations. The Beekeepers and Poultry Farmers cooperatives in Bullet Tree Falls were exceptions to the rule, achieving success because they implemented solutions that were in no way related to grand theories or the expectations of external funding agencies, and instead conformed to the norms already existing in the fabric of village culture. Despite their success, they received little public recognition and even less attention from the Department of Cooperatives or any other branch of the Belizean government. Their accomplishments and organizational innovations deserve discussion here.

The Beekeepers Cooperative

Two congenial brothers belonging to an immigrant family from Lebanon set up the Beekeepers Cooperative in 1979. Don Eduardo, the brother who led the business and organizational effort, knew almost nothing about honey production, but effectively used his skill in managing interpersonal relations in the context of village culture. I asked Don Eduardo how he happened to be so adept in interacting with people:

> It comes from something we have developed by talking to people, by—I think we Espats [his family name] have a certain amount of judgment. We are used to sitting down with people and solving problems. People come to us all the time. At 89 [years of age] I am a commissioner of the Supreme Court; I am a Justice of the Peace still.

Don Beto praised Don Eduardo for showing respect to people from diverse backgrounds, and he noted that others gave him respect in return. In one cooperative meeting observed by Don Beto, Eduardo made it a point to go around the room and ask every single member to offer his opinion about how the cooperative was functioning and suggest ideas about how things could be improved.

Unlike donor-driven projects that gave little or no consideration to markets, Don Eduardo's beekeeping project began with his visit to the business sections of the English and French embassies to find potential foreign purchasers for his product. Next he rounded up international donors, the U.S. Agency for International Development (USAID) being the most prominent, to provide grants to cover his costs in purchasing necessary equipment that included wooden boxes for honeycombs, a honey filtration system, and bottles for storing and transporting the honey. Don Eduardo's continuing role in the cooperative was to normalize its routines, oversee the marketing, and run the meetings.

Eduardo's younger brother, Don Gustavo, was equally comfortable in dealing with people (Figure 4.7). He owned a small grocery store, which was not a very lucrative business, but it provided a place where he had plenty of leisure to sit and "hold court," as neighbors, friends, and new visitors to the community dropped by to chat. He was easygoing, listened attentively, and made everyone feel respected.

Don Gustavo's assets were technical as well as interpersonal. He had received a U.S.-funded scholarship to enroll in a course on the science of beekeeping, held at a university in Ohio. His role in the Beekeepers Cooperative was to train, evaluate,

© Andrew Gordon

Figure 4.7 Don Gustavo, a leader of the Beekeepers Cooperative.

and support members on technical matters, such as hygiene, the use of antibiotics and pesticides, and the need to quarantine or eliminate any sickly portion of the bee population. The cooperative consisted of seven beekeepers from Bullet Tree Falls and three or four others from San Ignacio. During the months of April, May, and June, they brought their honeycombs to Gustavo's place to filter their honey, after which Gustavo evaluated the processed product for proper clarity and humidity and weighed the output. Workers then bottled the honey for transport and sale, receiving their checks on the spot as soon as their work was done, not waiting in limbo for a percentage of the sales, as was the procedure in donor driven cooperatives.

The beekeepers cooperative thrived until 1985, when, as reported by anthropologist Anne Southerland (1998: 147), the U.S. Drug Enforcement Administration (DEA) began spraying paraquat, a powerful herbicide, all over the Belizean countryside to knock out marijuana cultivation. The paraquat also killed flowers; without flowers as their food source, the bees died.

The Poultry Farmers' Cooperative

The Poultry Farmers' Cooperative, established in 1985, also arose from a local initiative in Bullet Tree Falls, thanks to the efforts of its leader Doña Sara and her son-in-law Niles Samuels. Critical to Doña Sara's success was arranging for marketing outlets where her cooperative could sell processed chickens to individual buyers, hotels, and retail stores in urban areas of Belize. One trait that served her well was her grit and determination acquired over many years of hard work, raising 13 children without any help from a non-supportive mate. All ten members of her cooperative attested to her exacting standards, clear communications, and hard work. She knew exactly how to deal with each member—setting rules, being fair, and praising each one's contribution. In conversing with Doña Sara several times at her home, I noticed that she spoke directly, in a matter-of-fact manner, with complete self-assurance. Her communication skills and reassuring demeanor must have impressed individual and institutional donors who provided initial funding for chicken coops and machines for de-feathering and cleaning slaughtered birds. At the same time she did not let donors dictate how she managed the cooperative.

Members of the cooperative individually raised their own batch of chickens in coops adjacent to their homes. After buying baby chicks, they nourished them until they reached a weight of about three pounds, at which time they slaughtered the birds and carried them to cooperative headquarters at Doña Sara's place to proceed with de-feathering, cleaning, and freezing. Before the task of plucking feathers became a mechanized operation, members had to report to headquarters at 2:30 in the morning to begin the work of processing. They took turns bringing in their birds on successive mornings; in other words, Doña Jeanette's chickens would be processed on one morning, Doña Betty's on another morning, and so on. As in the case of the Beekeepers Cooperative, Doña Sara paid her members on the spot after the processing of all birds was complete. Since all the women worked together in the processing, punctuality and diligence were mandatory. If a member missed participating in the early-morning work sessions, became less interested, or arrived with birds that were less than adequate size, Doña Sara would encourage her to change her ways. If problems persisted, Doña Sara would ask the woman to leave the cooperative. Doña Sara encouraged individual work and autonomy, very important aspects of village culture, as long as members followed the rules of the cooperative organization.

Niles Samuels worked in a full-time job for an NGO, but still assisted his mother-in-law on his own time. He originally gave Doña Sara the idea of raising chickens, pointing out that she could purchase baby chicks inexpensively from several Mennonite hatchery farms located in nearby Spanish Lookout. His initial role was to teach members about poultry diseases, infections, eating patterns, and the lighting of coops. Later his continuing role was to visit members' farms to answer questions and offer technical advice and encouragement. Niles arranged for each member to have an outlay of 50 chickens each, then 100, then several hundred, and finally 700. This gradual approach allowed members to absorb a steady, but not overwhelming flow of new information to put into practice. In this way farmers mastered the techniques of raising chickens in a step-by-step process as they increased production. Not a typical NGO employee, Niles was patient and supportive over a long period of time.

In 2002, the Poultry Cooperative folded when competitors with advanced machines for de-feathering began to sell their birds at cheaper prices. In existence for 17 years, Doña Sara's cooperative had turned a good profit, covering high school and college costs for 14 children of its members.

Ingredients for Success

The two cases of locally generated cooperatives offer contrasts to donor driven cooperatives that give us insight into the ingredients for success:

1. During the vast majority of their time, members worked individually, as was customary in Bullet Tree Falls, only working collectively for a few days during the final processing to prepare the product for transport to market. Their work had meaning because it reflected the desire for individual excellence, a significant element defining status and prestige in the culture of the *milpero*. These two cooperatives were not "cooperative" except in very limited circumstances, which enabled them to avoid the suspicions, conflicts, and flouting of the rules commonly found in donor driven cooperatives.
2. Leaders took the initiative to encourage and retain members who developed skills necessary to make the cooperative work, not just relying on family members to fill membership quotas and allowing them to work or not work as they pleased.
3. Leaders commanded respect due to their skills in dealing with people— maintaining fairness in setting and enforcing rules, offering encouragement to everyone, and listening to the opinions of workers in managing the organization.
4. Leaders arranged for marketing products as a hands-on practical matter before workers began to produce the products. Markets were not an afterthought left to

fate as they were in the onward march toward social justice or in the magical workings of capitalism.

5. The integrity and sustainability of business operations were not dependent on external stimulus provided by donor agencies. Cooperative members received some assistance from outside their community, yet they maintained complete autonomy in their operations, sustained by a sense of responsibility internal to the organization and tied to the success of their endeavor.

6. Leaders paid members immediately to reward them after processing the products they brought to headquarters, not waiting for the vagaries of sales and calculations of percentages of revenue to be returned later.

7. Workers benefitted from the technical expertise of highly skilled trainers, who also had effective interpersonal skills. Their training and support was not confined to the initial phase, but continued throughout the life of the cooperative.

Mentoring

Mentoring was an especially important ingredient in contributing to the success of the two locally generated cooperatives; a caring, person-to-person approach by leaders and technical experts motivated workers, kept them focused, and enhanced their natural cultural inclination to achieve individual excellence. The act of mentoring involves the generosity of spirit portrayed in the character named Mentor in Greek mythology. Sometimes Mentor took the form of an earthly being and at other times a heavenly spirit. In Homer's *Odyssey*, Athena, Zeus's daughter, sent the spirit Mentor to encourage Odysseus in the necessary task of getting rid of the suitors his wife had attracted while he was fighting battles in the Peloponnesian Wars. In another part of Homer's tale, the spirit Mentor emboldened Odysseus's son, Telemachus, to press on through hardship and adversity to win a major battle.

Understanding the fundamental process of mentoring does not require intensive schooling in Homeric epics. The support, encouragement, and progressive adoption of responsibility associated with mentoring are akin to basic features of family life, resembling exchanges that ideally occur between parents and children, the former nourishing the development of the latter. In our own lives, we are the outcome of paternal agents, mother and father figures who, if we are lucky, will help us, show us the way, guide us, do for us what we cannot, and continue in this fashion until we can do for ourselves.

The idea of mentoring usually applies to educational and business settings, but rarely to development projects such as cooperatives. I did manage to find one article on mentoring that summarizes its critical importance to various kinds of organizations. It was written for a newsletter with an audience of women employed by the federal government in Canada. Though aimed at a specialized group of workers, the article nevertheless has broad applicability to any setting. Quite unaware that her words would find meaning in Belize, author Janet B. Pilcha summarizes the value of mentoring:

> One of the best ways to help a person fulfill his or her potential within an organization is through the mentoring process. Studies have shown mentorship to be related to career

satisfaction and progress. The planned and structured guidance and sharing of knowledge and experience by effective supervisory or senior staff members can be a very
important aspect in the program's development of junior staff members. A mentor,
through repeated modeling and feedback, can shape a mentee's expectations, perceptions and ... behaviors (2011: 1).

To mentor is to promote the best in another person, and in Bullet Tree Falls, mentoring elevated members in two locally generated cooperatives to a high level of
performance.

THE LIMITATION OF IMAGINATION

I find it useful to think of a cooperative as an "imagined community"—that is, a
political, economic, and social ideal that springs from someone's mind. In 1983,
political scientist Benedict Anderson introduced the term "imagined communities"
in his book of the same title. He examines the designs of political leaders attempting to organize a diversity of people into a nation-state with shared identity and
common loyalty. His insights are applicable to the ways we have come to understand various kinds of human organizations, everything from large multinational
corporations to tribal groups, secessionist movements, and social experiments that
involve implementing new institutional forms, such as cooperatives. "Imagination"
is a useful word because it emphasizes that a cooperative is a construct of the mind,
shared by two or more persons, and therefore cultural, emanating from a particular
cultural context where pre-existing assumptions about right ways and wrong ways
of doing things become part of the design for realizing the intended ideal. Thus, in
order to understand the dynamics surrounding the introduction of cooperatives, I
have examined the relevant history and cultural practices in Canada deriving from
Catholic ideals of social justice and secular ideals about free-market capitalism. I
have likewise examined the history and cultural practices of the village of Bullet
Tree Falls. Disparate cultures containing conflicting assumptions generated resis-
tances at work, outside and inside the village, contain conflicting assumptions,
which generate resistance among villagers to externally imposed change. The conflicting assumptions, as I have shown, include attitudes, beliefs, habits, values,
behavioral norms, and ways of thinking about money.

Examining the cooperative movement has caused me to seriously think about
the many challenges created when imagination and ideology become the organizing
principles for institutional change. The promotion of goodwill and technical competence as means to solve problems and improve the human condition around the
world seems axiomatic, but this benign abstraction might find little traction once
touching down in the cultural context of an actual village such as Bullet Tree
Falls. Socialism and capitalism are ideologies that shape people's worldviews and
behavior, particularly in a political context, but neither one represents a sufficient
practical design to export as a means of bringing about economic and social development. What feels like a natural or more human way of organizing production in
one culture can feel like the complete opposite in another. Ironically, in the absence

of imported designs and ideology, two locally generated cooperatives out-performed those that were dreamed up elsewhere and transplanted into the community.

Not unlike what villagers in other parts of the world have done when they felt inadequately compensated for participating in foreign schemes, residents of Bullet Tree Falls resisted change. The support they received from external agencies that provided training and education was not sufficient beyond the start-up phase. Constrained by lack of time and personnel, funding agencies were ineffective agents of change, unable to get involved and straighten out the dysfunctional aspects of cooperative life. They neither fully recognized nor found a way to deal effectively with interpersonal conflicts and cultural incompatibilities that scuttled cooperative projects. In sum, intellectual and material transactions between the agents and recipients of change tended to be superficial or unsatisfactory.

How could things have been done differently to develop a successful cooperative program? The two cooperatives that developed without external stimulus—the beekeepers and poultry farmers—provide models of how successful cooperatives should operate. However, over a period of three decades, the emergence of indigenous, homegrown forms of cooperatives happened only twice in Bullet Tree Falls and affected only a small segment of the community. The role of outside sources in designing and funding cooperatives seems critical to carrying out the process of cooperative development on a large scale involving the lives of many villages and villagers. For this path of development to be successful, the formulation of an imagined community would have to be rethought to base it on broad community support, designs compatible with local cultural realities, and the involvement of villagers in planning and organizing. Change agents would need to be involved in the local community on a long-term basis, attentive to its cultural orientations, aware of problems as they arise, able to arrange for workers to have ongoing mentors, and ready to be critical of their own shortcomings and cultural biases.

5/Converts for Evangelicals[1]

In 1960, everyone living in the village of Bullet Tree Falls was Catholic, but by 2010, only 50 villagers still loyal to the Catholic Church showed up regularly for mass. In the 1970s, Bullet Tree Falls had become the target of missionaries from Evangelical religious sects in the United States. Over a period of four decades these sects accumulated around 800 followers, who were separated by several differences into two groups—Pentecostals and Social Gospel Evangelicals. Despite differences that I will discuss in this chapter, they were united by their emphasis on achieving personal transformation by accepting Jesus Christ as savior (see Figure 5.1 for a map showing the distribution of churches).

THE EVANGELICAL MESSAGE

Evangelicals brought the "news," called *evangel* in Greek, alerting people to the great benefits or the dire consequences that would follow from accepting or not accepting Jesus Christ as their savior. I attended many services in the various Evangelical churches in Bullet Tree Falls. In interacting often with pastors and other church leaders, I felt the power of their persuasive efforts intended to bring me into the fold. The Pentecostals gave me a most serious wake-up call. I recall how one pastor put his hand on my shoulder, looked me in the eye, and promised me that I was destined to burn forever in hell, unless I got busy and became a "real Christian" by accepting Jesus Christ, an act of volition that would bring me ever-lasting life in a heavenly paradise. Though the admonitions of other pastors were less scary, they repeated the same theme about accepting Jesus Christ, which meant maintaining the total absence of sin, adhering to the absolute authority of the Bible, and embracing the duty of all Christians to spread the news about Jesus. This refrain was constantly reinforced in church services usually held three to five times per week, and in casual interactions outside of church.

Evangelical missionaries in Bullet Tree Falls concentrated on an often repeated two biblical accounts they regarded as essential. One story from the Book of Revelations gave a terrifying description of the end of times and the ushering in of new divine order. The Book of Revelations in general is full of mind-expanding imagery and metaphors with accounts of the four horsemen of the apocalypse, plagues, a seven-headed beast, and dragons. It warns us about the moment of judgment that we all must face when we will be held accountable for our sins. After Jesus makes his "Second Coming" to earth, God will judge how righteously each of us has lived and determine who is entitled to salvation. Those fortunate enough to be saved will have everlasting life in heaven, while the rest will perish

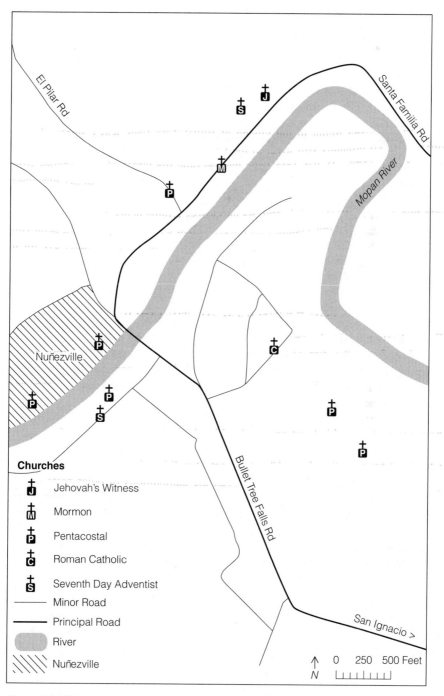

Figure 5.1 Village center—churches.

in a fearful outcome, described differently from church to church, perhaps burning in a lake of fire or simply suffering the erasure of one's soul.

Another favorite story of the Evangelicals, found in the Book of Genesis, was the familiar tale of Noah's Ark, interpreted by pastors as a metaphor for what will happen in the end times, when God will wash away all sins and sinful thoughts from the earth. The pastors warned villagers that they were living in the time of Noah and soon would face the same kind of judgment that came at the time of the great flood. God let only the righteous live on, that is, Noah and his family, who stayed high and dry in their ark. The rest of humankind, sullied by their lives of sin, washed away in the flood and perished from the earth.

Abolishing Alcohol and Sin

In Bullet Tree Falls, a life without sin meant no more drinking, dancing, and immodest behavior. The promise of the imminent coming of the judgment day gave women new ammunition to keep their husbands out of the bars, while men who converted followed their new moral compass to do the same. Before Evangelicals arrived in the village, wives often suffered from the irresponsible behavior of their husbands. Dinora, Pastor Arturo Macias's wife, told me about the widespread problem of drunken husbands squandering family money on alcohol. Her own husband's drunkenness began just one day a week and then increased to three days a week. "I would make remarks, and he'd get real angry with me, and hit me." She continued, "My husband would come home drunk three days after receiving a paycheck, all of the money spent, and I'd have nothing." But she was persistent and further explained:

> I asked the Lord to make him change. I was so tired of suffering. I said to myself, Arturo will change, Arturo will conform; the worldly desire will leave him, all these sinful worldly places. I prayed to God, and He changed things.

Arturo's change of heart occurred at the same time Dinora singled out his drinking as the cause of her coming down with tuberculosis, an illness so debilitating that she was unable to perform housework and take care of their children. Then Arturo "saw the light," started praying, and stopped drinking, he experienced a liberating transformation that eventually led him to become a pastor himself. Another village woman told a similar story: "Ramon used to come home with rice, beans, and sugar; the rest [of the money] went to fatten the owner of the bar." Then he turned to religion and his home life became considerably better.

Sometimes men prodded other men to change their ways. Don Roberto found sobriety and repented for his drunkenness and habit of getting into bar fights after his brother kept urging him to set a better example for his sons. Roberto submitted to his brother's wishes and later admitted his shame to his wife for squandering their money.

Conrado's life changed radically on March 8, 1997, when he was 26 years old. (Not uncommonly, he and other converts remember the exact date when they reached their epiphany.) Up to that time, he had led a wild life, drinking heavily while playing music in the bars with his band, the Silver Stars. He informed me that the band had specialized in ballads, meringue, salsa, and drunken weekends. After one wild binge, he suffered from physical trauma marked by symptoms of paralysis and trembling, leaving him unable to climb out of a hammock. At that moment he realized that the Lord was speaking to him, issuing a warning that he had to change his ways or die. He turned to abstinence, followed the life of Christ, and became a prominent Pentecostal missionary preaching at various venues in Cayo.

Religious interdictions by Evangelicals against alcohol abuse had a salutary effect on family life, reducing marital discord and allowing fathers to spend more time with their children. Family members ate better; bought better household furnishings such as beds, furniture, and kitchenware; and felt that their lives were improving overall.

Disappearing Spiritual Protectors

Catholic rituals and celebrations, once so much a part of village life, had been built on stories about saintly people, spiritual protectors of the village, and supernatural forces that watched over the village. All villagers participated in annual celebrations, a kind of village-wide party known as the *Fiesta Patronal* (Patron Festival). The purpose of this festival was to summon the protection of a religious force, the mercy inherent in the Trinity as it was embodied in the Cross of Santa Cruz, in a fiesta held on May 3. The village also held four other *fiestas* to recognize the spiritual presence of historical figures who still watched over them: the Virgin Mother on December 3; the Virgin of Guadalupe, the local embodiment of the Virgin in Mexico, on December 12; the Boy of Atocha (*Niño de Atocha*), known for showing mercy to prisoners and other great kindnesses, on February 2; and Saint Anthony, known for protecting people from all kinds of difficulties, on June 12. These festivals provided the opportunity for lay people to fulfill public ceremonial obligations and reinforced the social bonds that held villagers together in a faith shared by all.

Each festival represented the culmination, on the last day of a nine-day period of observance called a *novenario.* The first eight days were dedicated to prayer in appreciation of the protector, followed by the ninth day of exuberant celebration, organized and hosted by respected members of the village who provided food, drink, and entertainment. Villagers referred to hosts of the festivals as "owners" (*dueños*), elsewhere in Mesoamerica known as *mayordomos*), of the celebration. The "owners" also were responsible for guarding the sacred images of the village, usually consisting of pictures of the protectors. The village of Bullet Tree Falls had more than the usual number of protectors and festivals because it had more waves of immigrant groups, from Mexico and Guatemala, each requiring its own protector.

After Evangelicals began to dominate religious life in the village, the festivals either disappeared or became quite small, attracting only a few participants. Evangelicals denounced the celebrations as frivolous, pagan, idolatrous, sinful, not supported by any mention in the Bible, and clearly outside of Christian tradition. They deplored the drinking and the dancing that were part of the festivals, and they succeeded in humiliating the other villagers, the Catholics, discouraging their public expression of the these rituals of their faith, what had been symbols of common identity in the community.

Abandoning their protectors amounted to a major paradigm shift in people's minds about how to maintain the welfare of the community. Honoring protectors had been a part of Catholic tradition in Central American life for more than 500 years. Even earlier in their history the Maya practiced rituals to honor indigenous community protectors, normally manifest in the form of local deities. After the Spanish Conquest in the Sixteenth through the Eighteenth Centuries they swapped out their own Maya deities for Catholic saints. In many locations the swap was a seamless act of substitution in replacing one set religious figures with another. The Spanish conquerors adhered to the sixth-century dictum of Pope Gregory to destroy local temples devoted to "pagan gods" and replace them on the same site by constructing churches housing proper effigies of Catholic saints.[2] The historic attachment to village protectors had deep roots, both indigenous and Catholic roots; they were fundamental to how people lived and understood their very existence.[3]

Lost Rituals and Estranged Families

Accepting the Evangelical lifestyle cast former Catholics adrift from the historic ways of their ancestors even though they still lived in the same ancestral village. Don Arnoldo, the principal of the village's Catholic elementary school, referring to his own family, commented that the Evangelicals had " ... screwed up the culture. We were together, and they separated us. Because of this, we're all split up today." He was no longer in communication with some family members who had left the Catholic Church to become Mormons and Pentecostals. Upon overhearing our conversation, a friend of Don Arnoldo echoed the same theme: "Now each person follows a different way; they do not adore the Lord the same. One has his church here, another there. Otherwise, we might all be together."

Doña Susana Noh, a woman in her eighties, fondly recalled the festivals that she had enjoyed in her youth and lamented their loss. With a sad demeanor, she showed me the palm leaf replica of the Cross of Santa Cruz, which had been the focus of one of her beloved festivals that no longer existed. Her daughter had rescued the palm crucifix from a trash bin outside Tomas Tzib's store. Don Tomas, the owner of the store, no longer needed it after he had joined the Evangelicals.

Another lost ritual, called to my attention by my landlady and Charlie's mother, Doña Mirta, was the *Primicias*, or the Day of the Dead (*Dia de Los Muertos*) that took place annually on October 31 and November 1. Villagers turned out for this event to honor their dead ancestors, mostly parents and grandparents, by carrying their favorite foods to the cemetery to present them as offerings. Doña Mirta lamented that loss of this ritual, a loss that had eroded the social bonds between cousins who shared the same grandparents. Doña Mirta spoke wistfully about the warmth and friendship she felt when neighbors and friends enjoyed baking and sharing food during the *Posadas* celebration, held nine days before Christmas. At this time villagers welcomed visitors into their homes and offered them treats, reenacting the hospitality that the Three Wise Men received on their way to the manger, the site of Jesus's birth in Bethlehem.

Doña Mirta also mentioned that parents no longer concerned themselves with arranging for co-parent or godparent (*compadrazgo*) ties traditionally recognized to mark the birth, baptism, or marriage of a child. When a parent asked a trusted friend or kinsman to serve as a godparent, it added to the parental support available to the child and strengthened social bonds between families. According to the Evangelicals, co-parenting was a pagan custom, not properly Christian, and perhaps even an example of the work of Satan.

THE PENTECOSTALS

By 2010, Pentecostals had attracted 400 steady church members in Bullet Tree Falls, about half the total number of Evangelicals. Pentecostals were distinctive because of their ecstatic, consciousness-altering form of worship, in contrast to Social Gospel Evangelicals who relied on inspiration, not ecstasy, to reinforce the commitment of worshippers. The fervor created by Pentecostal missionaries and their converts affected just about every aspect of life in the village.

In Pentecostal church services worshippers reenacted eyewitness accounts of the Pentecost as described in the Bible (Acts Chapter 2) by Jesus's disciple, Luke:

> When the time for Pentecost was fulfilled, they were in one place together. And suddenly there came from the sky a noise like a strong driving wind.... Then there appeared to them as tongues as of fire, which parted and came to rest on each of them. And they were all filled with the Holy Spirit and began to speak in different tongues, as the Spirit enabled them to proclaim.

In his account of the Holy Spirit sent down to earth by Christ during the ninth day after he had ascended to Heaven, Luke observed that the 120 people who witnessed this event looked drunk, which was odd, he suggests, because it was only nine o'clock in the morning. At this point Luke realized that these witnesses acted and sounded strange because they were among "the saved," they entered what we now call an "altered state of consciousness."

My introduction to the Pentecostal world of Bullet Tree Falls began during a walk in the village when I noticed the construction of the new Emmanuel Church. While Pedro was hammering boards together, building the frame, I inquired, "Why build a new church when there are so many already?" Pedro answered my questions: "Shouldn't we have as many churches as *cantinas* (bars)?" A good answer, I thought, but later I learned that churches already far outnumbered bars—eleven churches to four bars. The more churches the better, Pedro added, "to lift up the community."

A Church Service Rocks

That same evening, I joined the Emmanuel Church congregation to observe the worship service. At 7:00 P.M., Pentecostal girls, boys, women, and men, many with Bibles in hand, walked calmly to church with no special look of anticipation and no special go-to-church clothing. Most of them came dressed in their work clothes—men with nothing fancier than tee shirts and work pants, and women with casual blouses and skirts. In contrast to their subdued demeanor outside the church, I was overwhelmed by the energy of the sound coming from inside the church; even from a distance it breathed excitement. A Christian rock band was warming up, reminding me of a club scene where an observer might walk in and encounter drinking, dancing, and revelers seeking to hook up. The musical genre was *cumbia*, popular in the country of Colombia, recognizable by its dreamy long notes underscored by a deliberate beat, evoking images of hips swaying from side to side. Its siren-like melodies seemed to yearn for attachment.

Worshippers entered a small sanctuary that had room for only ten rows of seats, and sat down wherever they chose, young people grouping themselves together apart from married couples and single adults. Inside the church, the sounds affected me differently; I could hear worshippers shouting their praise and love for Jesus, offering testament to how Jesus had made a great difference in their lives. What I was hearing was the preparation of bodies and psyches for a transcendental moment, provoking an altered state of consciousness, soon to arrive.

Transcendental moments are a worldwide phenomenon, constituting a part of many religious traditions, including monotheistic Jews and Muslims, who on some occasions experience spiritual ecstasy, as do believers in polytheistic religions such as Hinduism and followers of animistic religions involving shamanism.

I watched intently as Pedro took charge of the Pentecostal service, guiding his congregation on a spiritual journey, its formulaic character defining it as a cultural ritual, in which all the actors know the general format. I was struck by the sensuous undertones to the warm-up driven by erotic-sounding music, not for sex, but for the love of God. After 20 minutes the band abruptly stopped playing cumbia music and transitioned into the Norteño style of Northern Mexico, a polka and rock mixture that invites fast, joyful dancing. Worshippers enthusiastically followed the beat and shouted praises to the Lord, "Gloria!" and "Hallelujah!".

After another 10 minutes interspersed with several short readings from the Bible, the music took a step down in rhythm, into a slower ballad form. The shift in pace had its intended psychological effect. Anthropologist Michael Winkelman (2009: 385–428) writes about how music mobilizes spiritual experiences. Initially fast music charges up the sympathetic nervous system, raising blood pressure, heart rate, and mental acuity. Then a slow tempo mobilizes the parasympathetic nervous system, creating a relaxing effect that leaves the listener susceptible to suggestion. At this point, Pedro offered praise to Jesus in poetic form; it seemed as if his poetry had become the lyrics for the melodies churned out by the church band. All of the musicians in the band were Pedro's children, two playing guitars, along with two others on a keyboard and one setting the beat on several drums. I listened to Pedro sing along with the instrumentals as I recorded his words.

Jesus who can do everything

You who are so close

Although we cannot see him, we can feel him

We adore you, Christ our Lord.

We wait for your call

It does not matter when.

I'm always ready

To be in the royal palace you provide.

A Formula for Ecstasy

After this short song of adoration, the music sped up again with repetitive percussion rhythms. Worshippers looked restless and began to stomp their feet, some almost dancing in their seats. Michael Harner tells us that repetitive drumbeats of the shaman, or perhaps any drumbeats, can induce an altered state of consciousness by firing up the brain's theta waves to produce a kind of out-of-body experience. I continued to observe as worshippers launched a sequence of hand gestures in four stages, each one progressing closer to the Lord:

Stage I: Fingers point in the direction to the Lord

Worshippers raised their right hands and pointed their elbows and index fingers forward, bending their forearms forward with each beat of the drum, and then began chanting "to you, to you" (*a ti, a ti*), with their fingers pointing to Heaven and the Lord as their destination.

Step II: Windshield wipers

Raising the left arm next to the right arm with palms spread flat and open, they faced the front of the church. Their forearms swiveled to the left 45 degrees and then to the right 45 degrees, moving from side to side like a windshield wiper, a gesture to symbolize how the presence of the Lord is vast and worldwide. Shouts of praise—"Gloria" and "Hallelujah"—accompanied these movements, while worshippers remained attentive to the pastor who would signal the next step.

Step III: Climbing the ladder

As worshippers continued their chants of praise, they pushed their hands higher with their fingers curled as if they were about to wrap them around the next rung of a ladder, another step higher and closer to God. The cadence of the music suggested that this was a step-by-step process, plodding along, as worshippers asked for mercy and love from the Lord. The ladder suggested a straight path to the Lord, but still involved a climb that required effort.

Step IV: Knocking on Heaven's Door

Worshippers raised both hands, as high as possible, and clenched their fists, thrusting them forward, again and again, as if banging on a door, while they shouted praises and pleaded for mercy. Bob Dylan's song "Knockin' on Heaven's Door," also performed by Bruce Springsteen, Bob Marley, Bon Jovi and countless others, played in my mind. The worshippers had reached the threshold, about enter the door and summon the Holy Spirit.

Glossolalia

(vocalizing speech-like syllables often lacking in conventional meaning, yet conveying a sacred language).

Felicitas Goodman, an anthropologist who did fieldwork with Maya Pentecostals in the Yucatan, noted how they communicate with the Holy Spirit in the same way that shamans seek their guardian spirit, by using what one scholar of shamanism called "archaic techniques of ecstasy."[4] The physical sensations resulting from exertion, pain, dancing, fasting, etc., are sufficient to induce an altered state of consciousness. For the Pentecostals in Bullet Tree Falls, it was music, hand gestures, and drumming that turned longing into ecstasy. As I watched that evening, the Pentecost was replicated in Emmanuel Church. Dinora, the pastor's wife, stepped forward, appearing to be emotionally overwrought, and began speaking in tongues what is formally called glossalallia. Here are some of her typical utterances:

Arabba-allaba-saba-allababa si alaba, rabatamba alasoh

Feel my presence, said the Lord

Oh rabasaika, rabalaba uribacando alabasica tacabalacaisoca,

I am here rabacacanda ribisaica

The power of the Lord is here.

Her words came out in clumps of sound seeming to originate from her body as well as her mouth. In the process of making such sounds, Pentecostals believe the body becomes a vessel for the Holy Spirit, the same as it did for the 120 witnesses described by Luke in the Bible.

Dinora's performance was mysterious and full of power. She spliced phrases of regular language (for instance, "feel my presence" and "I am here") into her speaking in tongues, which suggested that the glossolalia was necessary to fully verify the Lord's presence in this particular place at this particular time. Although her glossolalia never included the word "*alabanza*," (meaning praise or worship in Spanish), she got the point across by using repeated approximations, "*alas*" and "*allabas*." Keeping the full and clear articulation of "*alabanza*" just barely out of reach conveyed the importance of using a special spiritual language to express the real power of the Lord's presence and love. Other sounds in Dinora's glossolalia were associated with giving comfort to worshippers, for example, "*rabas*" and "*alabas*" are bi-labial utterances used by Spanish-speaking mothers try to lull children to sleep with soothing sounds.

After a several-minute pause in the proceedings, it was time for the "altar call," when all worshippers walked up the aisle to the altar. Teenage girls showed the most emotion, advancing with arms around each other, crying and swaying from side to side. Dinora resumed speaking in tongues, touched each person's head, and spoke words of comfort, "Heal with the power of Christ."

After the altar call, Pastor Arturo came forward to signal the end of the service; it was already past 10:00 P.M. when people needed to go home. He recapped the evening, reaffirming that the Holy Spirit had visited, and that we should all be thankful. The band brought the worshippers back to "the real world" by playing the same *cumbia* music that had welcomed them into the church. The music and the memory of their experience that night would beckon them to return, to be in touch with the Lord, when they again would be uplifted on a spiritual journey.

Pentecostal Roots in America

The Pentecostal faith was already well established in the United States almost seven decades before it came to Bullet Tree Falls. In 1905, the Azusa Congregation, named after the small church on Azusa Street in Los Angeles, became one of the principal starting points for the Pentecostal movement.[5] William Seymour, of African-American background, ministered to a multi-racial congregation in an old frame building that formerly housed a Methodist church. A magnificently charismatic preacher, Seymour inveighed against racism, claiming that it detracted from giving glory to God, and that he embodied the spirit of the frontier experience as described by historian Fredrick Jackson Turner to embody the traits of independence, individualism, and personal industry. Turner's frontier traits closely match the ideals espoused by Pentecostal leaders.

> The ideal of discovery, the courageous determination to break new paths, indifference to dogma... [A] spirit of innovation" (Turner 1994 (1914): 154).

Seymour embraced this daring "frontier spirit" in his version of Christianity, which he believed was dramatically superior to the conformist and rational quality of mainstream Protestant churches. Seeking to spread the word, he created a template for conducting ceremonies, evoking emotions, implanting new ideas, and uplifting spirituality, easily copied by other pastors across the United States and around the world. In Seymour's church, members of his congregation pushed through a mental and social frontier. Blacks and Whites prayed together and swooned together, lost in devotion to God. They entered the zone of primordial spiritual feelings, which opened them a larger spiritual universe, where all beings could get in touch with the Holy Spirit. Clergy came from far and wide to visit the Azusa church and were enthralled with what they saw, inspired to return home to find new converts and hold their own revival services with music, lights, and prayers, leading to the ecstatic acceptance of Jesus and preparation for his second coming.

The Pentecostal movement arose at a moment in history when Americans wanted a livelier form of worship and a new spirituality that would break out of the staid ways of the Protestant churches that dominated American life. Pentecostals sought to achieve an undiluted adoration (*agape* in Greek) of God and Christ, as inspired by the writings of medieval Christian theologians. Harvey Cox, an eminent American theologian, wrote about William Seymour's zeal in his book *Fire from Heaven: The Rise of Pentecostal Spirituality and the Reshaping of Religion in the Twenty-First Century*:

> [Pentecostalism] would renew and purify a Christianity they believed was crippled by empty rituals, dried-up creeds, and the sin of racial bigotry ... when the fire did fall

[at Azusa Street] ... a spiritual fire roared forth that was to race around the world and touch hundreds of millions of people with its warmth and power (Cox 1996: 46-48, quoted in Anderson 2004: 44).[6]

In 1906, only one year after it had begun, the Pentecostal movement spread outside the United States, to eventually claim 100s of millions of adherents throughout the world (Wacker 1999: 27). By 1918, the *Pentecostal Herald* in the United States had reached an impressive circulation of 550,000 and was spreading news of the movement all over the country (Wilson 2001: 72). Offshoots of the early Pentecostal movement included the International Pentecostal Holiness Church, founded in 1911, and later made famous by Oral Roberts; the International Church of the Foursquare Gospel led by Aimee Semple McPherson, founded in 1923; and the Pentecostal Church of God founded in 1919. It was pastors from the Pentecostal Church of God who brought their faith to Bullet Tree Falls.

Tent Meetings Come to Bullet Tree Falls

American Pentecostal missionaries, driven by their independence and frontier spirit, came to Bullet Tree Falls in 1972. Villagers described how Rex and Roy Parnell, twin brothers from Oklahoma, along with their older brother Doyle Parnell rolled into town in their buses and organized tent meetings with all the trappings of flood-lights, music, and movies. Church services celebrating the Second Coming of Christ led up to mass conversions, as people exuberantly turned their lives over to God, singing tearfully and trembling as they accepted the gift of the Holy Spirit. Previously, evenings in the village had been very dark and quiet because it was without any electricity. The Parnell brothers supplied generators to power up light-ing, amplifiers, and projectors, using the light and sound to create excitement and attract villagers to their services, where they offered them free food, used clothes, and Bibles.

Realizing that an interview with the Parnell brothers would provide valuable historical information, I asked around the village to find out if anyone knew their street address or phone number in the United States, but to no avail. Fortunately, on a visit to San Ignacio, I ran into Brother James Golden, a rock-solid member of the Evangelical community in San Ignacio for 47 years. He was the in-country repre-sentative of the Pentecostal Church of God, and was still in touch with the Parnell brothers. He handed me the email address of Rex Parnell. After sending several introductory emails and responses, I received permission from Rex to travel to east-ern Oklahoma to meet him and his twin brother, Roy, who lived nearby.

In 2011, I met with the twin brothers, then 80 years old, and conducted separate interviews with both. Later, I went to a location near Oklahoma City to interview Edna Parnell, the widow of Doyle, the older brother who had died at the age of 80 in 2003. Visiting the homes of the three brothers destroyed my expectations of encountering rich and powerful preachers. They lived a life of very moderate means, travelling to conduct their international ministry with the support of money from the church. Rex and his wife Wilma had just returned from a month of missionary work in Uganda, while Roy and his wife Geraldine had just returned from Northern California, where they had staged five revival services in as many days.

At 80 years of age, Rex and Roy were still quite imposing in appearance, with big frames and big bellies, and they were eager to engage in conversation. Edna (Doyle's widow), in her mid-80s, appeared calmer. She no longer traveled, but was pleased to reflect on how the church and the Lord had provided for the spiritual welfare of Doyle's widow, Edna.

All three brothers lived in single-family houses, most likely built in the 1970s and typical of working-class residences. Two of the three structures consisted of connected, doublewide trailers, and the third, of standard construction, was of comparably small size. Thick polyester carpets covered the floors. Artifacts made of china, such as sculptures, plates, and bowls, were everywhere. I saw no signs of religious artifacts in any of the three houses, with the exception of one Bible lying on a table—no crucifixes, no images of Jesus and Mary, and no picture of the Last Supper. Their religion was internal, not external, but inside the body— the temple of the soul.

The brothers told me that they moved to Bullet Tree Falls because of a "burden" given to them by God, manifest and visible as if it were part of their bodies. Roy showed me the weight of the burden with his two hands stretched toward the front, palms facing one another, as if holding two sides of a chunky boulder. They had acquired the burden through Ernest Parnell, their father, who was born in Indian Territory before Oklahoma became a state. In the Pentecostal world, burdens often start with a vision, and Ernest's experience was no exception. As a young man, he had a dream that contained a message from God revealing that his life would be devoted to working with American Indians. In the dream he introduced himself to an elderly American Indian sitting on a curb, and invited him to a revival meeting where the Indian wholeheartedly accepted Jesus Christ as his savior. Baptism by the Holy Spirit marked Ernest's acceptance of the burden portrayed in a dream. He acquired the powers of healing in the same ceremony when Lord put a "fit" (an ecstatic state) on him. God had spoken; Ernest was destined to become a preacher.

Ernest carried his burden with a single-minded drive that challenged the patience and endurance of his family, but in equal measure inspired strangers who eagerly became his converts. In his book called *Just a Passin' Thru': The Story of the Ernest Parnell Family and Their Pioneering Traveling Ministry*, B. L. Hinkle, Ernest's nephew, describes how his family suffered from neglect, hunger, homelessness, and occasional hostility from a town that did not act kindly toward Pentecostals. Yet Ernest was unstoppable in his quest for converts, even when faced with a language barrier. Ernest's oldest son Doyle observed him in church preaching to a group of Spanish-speakers who could not understand English, while Ernest could not speak Spanish. Ernest kept on going, speaking neither in English nor in Spanish, but instead

In tongues, [he] stops, and asks, 'Comprende', one of his few Spanish words. First they say 'No comprende' and then he preaches in tongues again, and again asks 'Comprende?' And after three or four times, they say, 'Si' ... on the next night we have a whole building full of Spanish-speaking folks ... (Hinkle 2010: 37).

Afterwards, all the Spanish speakers made altar calls, proceeding to the front of the room to accept Jesus as their savior.

Hinkle reports that even after his death Ernest was relentless in transferring his burden to the next generation. Doyle described how his father reached out to him in a dream and urged him

> to take the mantle of his burden for the Indian and Spanish people ... [then on a following night] I look up at the dark sky and the clouds seem to open up in one spot and I see a great crowd of Indian and Spanish faces. So I know that I'm supposed to go to the mission fields and preach to the Indian and Spanish people (Hinkle 2010: 213).

Brothers Rex and Roy eventually joined Doyle. Rex started out on a very different path, taking part in a counterfeiting racket and coming close to committing murder. God intervened, telling Rex "even if you figure out how to get by man-made law, you can't get by God's law." Rex knelt and prayed, later recognizing that as the moment he "returned to the Lord and never left him again."

Hinkle brought a fourth brother to my attention, Guy, the youngest sibling and prodigal son in the Parnell family. Guy rebelled against his father by becoming a psychedelic rock musician with a taste for illicit drugs, but God intervened in his life as well. He had his own encounter with the Holy Spirit while Doyle, Roy, and Rex prayed "over him." Guy elegantly described this ecstatic experience.

> Blue light whips around me and goes through me, and I feel like somebody is pouring warm water through me and cleaning me out, and I'm not in the pit no more.... I realize I'm born again, and for the first time in my life I understand why Dad did what he did (Hinkle 2010: 211–212).

Converts in Bullet Tree Falls

In the beginning of their missionary careers, the Parnell brothers first sought converts among Spanish-speakers and American Indians in the southwestern United States, and from there they proceeded to carry their message to Bullet Tree Falls where it spread quickly. Brother James Golden explained to me their formula for success:

> First a missionary heats up the crowd with lights and sound, prayer song and music. Once they already come forward, you have them. After the meeting all those who have come forward feel like they will want to repeat the experience; they find each other. They get together; one of them leads and eventually forms a church.

Pastor Conrado, a local church member in Cayo, converted after temporary paralysis changed his taste in music and brought him to the Lord. Conrado describes the power of church music that

> ... connects the mind to the Lord, and one doesn't think of anything other than the blessings of the Lord. Music causes people to lose control of their thoughts. One feels one's body is on fire and the fire is lit in others, and that we're all children of God.

In Bullet Tree Falls, waves of Pentecostal fervor washed over the village after the Parnell brothers created a nucleus of converts. Enrique Nuñez, the most

Figure 5.2 Service at the Pentecostal Church where Enrique Nuñez was the founding pastor.

important figure in this nucleus, joined the Pentecostals at the age of 15 and started preaching in the early 1970s. He was fearless in evangelizing to a Catholic village then quite hostile to Pentecostals. Other Pentecostal missionaries who came after the Parnell brothers helped Enrique to start making actual converts. They urged him to move from the South Side of Bullet Tree Falls to Nuñezville, a section of the village where many residents shared his family name and where a small number of Pentecostal families already lived.

Enrique not only moved his residence as the missionaries had directed, but also started a church in Nuñezville, which became a hub of Pentecostal activity (Figure 5.2). His first converts were his own family members. Several years later, I discovered that 15 of the 25 households occupied by people with the Nuñez family name had converted to the Pentecostal faith. Enrique's church, named *Sendero de Luz* (the Path of Light), was the largest of all the Pentecostal churches in the village. Located at the entrance to Nuñezville, it could accommodate 300 worshippers at once. Proud of his work, Enrique showed me a list of his baptisms that included Don Beto's wife in 1980, Don Beto's two daughters in 1984, and many Nuñez family members. Much of the rest of the village soon experienced conversion through the same technique of bringing people into an ecstatic union with the Holy Spirit, and then sharing the experience with others. By the time I arrived to conduct fieldwork in 2009, the sounds and excitement of several Pentecostal churches pervaded the entire village. The excitement of the Pentecostal revival also captured the attention of the surrounding area of Cayo, with a radio station conveying the Pentecostal message in sermon and song, seven days a week (Figure 5.3).

Figure 5.3 The Pentecostal radio station now reaching all of Cayo.

The rise of the Pentecostal Faith in Bullet Tree Falls was without interruption, a fluid process as new converts continuously found inspiration in the ecstasy of the Holy Spirit. Originating in Oklahoma in 1905, the inspiration of a zealous family patriarch made its way through Indian country and onward to Belize in the succeeding generation, successfully applying its template for conversion in a completely different cultural setting. As Harvey Cox said, it was a "spiritual fire that roared forth."

SOCIAL GOSPEL EVANGELICALS—ADVENTISTS

Social Gospel Evangelicals were the second major Protestant group to bring radical change to the lives of villagers. Compared to Pentecostals, Social Gospel Evangelicals were far more rational and civic-minded, and not inclined to integrate ecstatic experiences into their religious ritual. They focused their attention on the salvation of society, with less concern for individual salvation. Seventh Day Adventists were the most prominent sect among Social Gospel Evangelicals in Bullet Tree Falls, numbering about 300 members; the other two groups, Latter Day Saints (Mormons) and Jehovah's Witnesses, each claimed about 50 members.

Here I will focus my discussion on the Seventh Day Adventists. Not only were they the largest of the three Social Evangelical groups in Bullet Tree Falls, their sizeable membership meant that they supported a full complement of specialized activities typical of Adventist churches, with programs designed for young people, adults, outreach to non-members, and community support. Although the three social gospel religions in general have common characteristics, as indicated previously, differences among them do exist and are important to insiders. For example, Adventists choose Saturday for the Sabbath, not Sunday. Mormons baptize the dead, a ritual the others would never accept. Jehovah's Witnesses focus on entering the Kingdom of God—a separate social-political order—whereas Adventists and Mormons seek to improve the order that already exists on earth. For our purposes, however, the most significant differences to consider are those between the Pentecostals and Social Gospel Evangelicals taken categorically.

Social Gospel Evangelicals emerged on the American religious scene in the mid-nineteenth century, when major social problems were obvious and growing. Rapid industrialization and urbanization of society brought terrible squalor, poor hygiene, alcohol abuse, disinterest in education, and dysfunctional families. The primary objective of Social Gospel Evangelicals was to make the possibility of salvation real, not for one individual at a time, but instead for an entire society.

A Blend of Traditions

Social Gospel Evangelicals blended two early American religious traditions, the first being the civic-mindedness of late eighteenth-century Congregationalist, Episcopalian, Presbyterian and Unitarian churches. Although their followers were relatively small in numbers, these churches maintained a dominant presence through using their moral compass to guide leaders in civic affairs. Their clergy were well educated, literate, and inquiring; in 1776, 57 percent were graduates of Harvard University and 26 percent were graduates of Yale University (Fink and Stark 1989: 40). Though ethical and socially involved, they were not very spiritual, in this way contrasting with Western and frontier culture that existed on the margins of civil society.

The early Protestant ministers in America were part of what Turner described as the extended elite cultural influence of London and its provinces in Montreal, Boston, New York, and Washington (1994: 218). The theological roots of Congregationalists, Unitarians, and Presbyterians were also political roots, as many legislators in colonial America and the early post-colonial era were part of church life that primarily adhered to ethical, as opposed to spiritual, commitments. Their culture was not at all like that of the Pentecostal world where experimentation, innovation, and adventure were prevalent.

Drawing upon the intellectual and civic-mindedness of the early Protestants, Social Gospel Evangelicals cultivated a literate and educated clergy who were equally committed to the improvement of society. One of the Adventist founders, Ellen White (1827–1915), who grew up in Portland, Maine, wrote 40 books as well as numerous educational materials and articles. Mormon leader Joseph Smith (1805–1844), originally from Vermont and then New York State, wrote a sacred text entitled *The Book of Mormon*, followed by two more books outlining Mormon philosophy, the *Pearl of Great Price* and *Doctrine and Covenants*. Jehovah's Witness leader Charles Taze Russell (1852–1916), originally from Pittsburgh, Pennsylvania, wrote a six-volume commentary on the Bible, *The Millennial Dawn*, as well as numerous articles, pamphlets, and sermons.

But they were different than their forbearers in being far more inspired by spiritual matters. A second tradition inherited by Social Gospel Evangelicals, a spiritual orientation derived from eighteenth and early nineteenth century Baptists and Methodists, the ones who emphasized spiritual awakening, feeling, and passion for worship. The popularity of Social Gospel Evangelical sects came from the tide of Baptist and Methodist spirituality while also maintaining the ethical and social posture of the New England sects. The Social Gospel enthusiasm drew on the spiritual vigor of "The Great Awakening" in American religion. Roger Finke and Rodney Stark (1989) chart the history of this Baptist and Methodists movements in a lively titled article "How the Upstart Sects Won America: 1776–1850." They describe how the Baptist and Methodist pastors drew attention to the "otherworldly" importance of the second coming, preaching about their faith in tent meetings and open field revivals, and reaching out to far flung communities by "circuit riding" from one place to another. They made inroads for Jesus in rural areas outside the urban centers of the Northeast.[7]

Baptist and Methodist churches tripled their membership during the period from 1776 to 1850. A great part of their success was due to their conferring moral worth on ordinary people and giving them hope for an afterlife. According to Finke and Stare, Baptists and Methodist ministers were a different breed than their counterparts in the ethically minded urban north. Only 11.5 percent of the Baptist pastors were college-educated, and the Methodists had no seminary for training pastors until 1847 (Finke and Stark 1989: 35–36). Baptist and Methodist ministers engaged in intense proselytizing to appeal to workers and farmers. They preached that the ways of the world familiar to most people were soon coming to an end, because sin had reached such an unbearable level that Jesus would soon return to earth to bring justice to the saved and punishment to the sinners.

In sum, the Social Gospel Evangelicals had a social conscience with the emphasis on education and civic involvement of Northeastern Protestants, combined with the spiritual passions of the Baptists and Methodists, but Social Gospel Evangelicals in Bullet Tree Falls (Adventists, Jehovah's Witnesses and Mormons) did not go as far as the Pentecostals in seeking the ecstasy of the Holy Spirit. Social Gospel religions were attentive to the second coming, but also admonished followers to reach for a higher ethical state, or to "cleanse the Sanctuary" in the words of Adventist leader Ellen White, whose stated goal was for humanity to prepare, not just wait, for the second coming (Morgan 2001: 13–14).

ENCOUNTERS WITH THE ADVENTIST WORLD

My first encounter with the Adventists came when I introduced myself to several teenage girls serving food at a snack bar, located just a few blocks from the Adventist church. They eagerly told me about their affiliation with the Adventists and an upcoming weekend camping event sponsored by their church. They planned to study the Bible, play games, and participate in mindful worship free from the corrupting influence of several young people in the village known to have started drinking alcohol and taking drugs—"a scourge in the village," they said.

Intrigued by what I had learned from the girls at the snack bar, I later arranged to visit another weekend camp that Adventists had set up for the teenagers of Cayo. The religious orientation of the event was evident in the way the organizers had structured a kind of ideal society. Though its existence was only temporary, the Bible camp served to convey a timeless message about how the teens should live—being thoughtful and mindful of the power of Jesus. Consistent with their rational objectives, the planners of the outing made sure that activities maintained a quiet tone, without any of the excitement characteristic of Pentecostal gatherings.

When I arrived in the middle of the afternoon, the campers were split into two teams competing with each other to answer challenging questions about stories from the Bible—for example: Who was the King of Azar? What day did Passover start? What did the spies tell Rahab have to do to save Jericho from destruction? According to Rahab, how did the people of Jericho feel about the Israelites? A correct answer earned applause; a wrong answer resulted in the emcee turning away to seek the answer from a camper on the other team. A final victory brought cheers from the winning side and polite clapping from the other. No sore losers were allowed here. After the game, all contestants gathered together to sing songs of praise, called "singspirations," followed by ice cream for everyone.

Campers set up individual tents for three nights in proximity to other campers from their home church and community, each cluster posting an outward facing sign to identify themselves according to their home church. Within each group of tents, they separated the sexes—boys on one side and girls on the other. In the midst of several hundred teenagers with raging hormones, I saw no romantic or intimate encounters, not even any flirtatious glances between boys and girls.

As I looked out over a stretch of the river on what had become a hot afternoon, I felt the urge to swim. Noticing that no one was in the water, I asked an adult bystander, "Why aren't the campers in bathing suits?"

"Dress codes," came the answer.

"Was this rule just for the Sabbath?" I asked.

"No, always," he told me. "Long pants are the rule. No swimming." He reasoned that sexual predators might want to have their way with young girls and reminded me that immodest exposure leads to adultery. I listened without comment. The young people clearly enjoyed the occasion and did not complain about the regulations keeping them out of the water. Life was orderly and calm in this temporary society of mindful teenagers, who exhibited an extraordinary amount of tranquility and self-control.

The Sacred Stories of Ellen White

Among the Adventists, only the founder and leader of the church, Ellen White, who spent most of her working life in the heart of America, Michigan, could enter into a special dialogue with God. Her experiences and orientation were brought to life in Bullet Tree Falls, over a century later.

Through nineteenth-century America, her visions, and sacred stories based on her inspirations, became legendary, laying the foundation for the two primary worldly missions of the faith—health and education. I learned about White from the works of scholars who spent their lives studying the Adventists, one being P. Gerard Damsteegt. In his book *Foundations of the Seventh-Day Adventist Message and Mission* (1977), he reports that White's inspiration with regard to health care started on Christmas Day 1865, when she had a vision that the church would become an instrument for health reform and the development of hospitals. Regarding health as connected to "the spirit of holiness," she regularly lectured about following a proper diet consisting mostly of grains and vegetables, and little if any meat, and no alcohol, tea, coffee, or tobacco. In 1866, she opened a health institution where Adventist physicians would treat all-comers regardless of their religious affiliation. White's strategy was to favorably impress patients with the healing powers of Adventist doctors, indirectly encouraging them to convert to the Adventist faith. White also expected Adventist patients to become instruments of outreach to other patients who were not yet Adventists. She wrote:

> Acquainted with Sabbath-keepers and our real faith, their prejudice is overcome, and they are favorably impressed. By thus being placed under the influence of the truth some will not only obtain relief from bodily infirmities, but their sin-sick souls will find a healing balm (White 1867: 53 quoted in Damsteegt 1977: 238).

Ronald Numbers, another scholar who admired White, authored the *Prophetess of Health: A Study of Ellen G. White* (2008). He gives White extensive credit for health initiatives that changed America. He reports that Ellen White collaborated with Dr. John Kellogg, the entrepreneur who created Corn Flakes and the first version of granola, to develop a 23-week course in basic health education, to establish a school to teach nursing and another to teach food hygiene, to introduce the use of massage therapy, and the use of electricity in healing. In 1910, White went on to establish a medical college (now the Loma Linda University Medical Center), currently featuring a medical school, hospital, behavioral health institute, and nursing school. By the time the Adventist church missionaries moved into Bullet Tree Falls in 1972, the Church had worldwide missionary accomplishments to build upon, including 140 hospitals staffed by 1,100 physicians and an even greater number of nurses and technicians.

White was interested in promoting specialized educational instruction along with general K–12 and university education. Her commitment to education was equally as strong as her commitment to health, and her plans in both fields were equally as lofty. One evening she had a vision instructing her to send "colporteurs," to serve as missionaries around the world and sell Adventist literature, consisting mostly of materials she had written. This unusual word, "colporteur," derives from the eighteenth-century Middle French word *comporteur*, meaning peddler. With an "l" inserted after "co" instead of an "m," the word then means "book peddler." I suppose adopting a French-sounding word lent more distinction to her endeavor than the common English word of peddler.

Her calling in education came in a vision she had in 1848, at the age of 21:

> After coming out of a vision, I said to my husband: I have a message for you. You must begin to print a little paper and send it out to the people. Let it be small at first.... From this small beginning it is shown to me to be streams of light that went round the world (White 1990: 1).

Five decades later she had not let up her determination. She wrote there could be no

> higher work than evangelistic canvassing [as a colporteur].... We must educate, educate, and educate young men to ... sell those.... [Our] presses now be constantly employed in publishing light and truth.... the publications set forth from our printing houses are to prepare a people to meet God. Through the world, they are to do the same work that was done by John the Baptist for the Jewish nation (White 1990: 1–19).

The Spirit of Ellen White is Revived in Bullet Tree Falls

The Adventists developed an extraordinary structure of religious education that enhanced their missionary work all over the world, and in Bullet Tree Falls. Wherever Adventists were present, colporteurs were present as well. The general education Adventists provided was equally widespread. By 1972, the year the Adventists arrived in Bullet Tree Falls, their accomplishments worldwide were already impressive; they had established 62 colleges, 83 secondary schools, and 914 elementary schools, along with 50 publishing houses turning out literature in 179 languages.

In the latter part of the twentieth century and in the first decade of the twenty-first century, the Adventist accomplishments in Belize were considerable, including the establishment of 21 elementary schools, five high schools, and one junior college. During the period of my field research, they expanded an elementary school in Bullet Tree Falls as well as increasing the size of several other schools elsewhere in the Cayo district. As well as religious education, Adventist schools offered education secular in orientation (reading, writing and arithmetic and so on). As well, they also spread the Adventist message about preparing for the second coming by living a clean Adventist life. This fusion of secular and religious education was compatible with the existing hybrid education system in Belize, in which churches built and administered primary and secondary schools, while the government covered teachers' salaries.

Corporate Organization of Adventists in Belize

The Adventist strategy of setting up health and education institutions was effective in spreading their religious message. Rational and hard-nosed in devising strategies for growth, they followed nineteenth-century business models adopted earlier and used successfully by Protestant sects. In his book *Protestants and American Business Methods* (1979), Ben Primer describes a trend among national church organizations headquartered on the east coast in the last third of the nineteenth century toward the use of formal accounting methods and marketing techniques to grow and expand; in short, they took on the mantel of the corporate model. For example, in 1898, the administrative body of the national Episcopalian church declared that it wanted to acquire "business system and method"; and in 1894, Methodist administrators were explicit about their need for "the conditions of business success" (1979: 72–73).

In contrast Belizean Pentecostals were completely decentralized without any coordinated planning. The Adventists adopted centralized authority, national advertising, annual reports and meetings, collection of statistics, and management controls on business functions, such as uniform pricing of books and other church merchandise. And this situation continued during my research.

The Pentecostal Church of God in Belize, an offshoot of the American Pentecostal Church of God, had scant organizational support, consisting of only one staffer located in Cayo, who received little support from church headquarters in the United States. He had no office, worked out of his own residence, and carried out only a few supervisory responsibilities, such as calling meetings and arbitrating disputes among members of a church. In the United States, the headquarters was no different. The Pentecostal Church of God headquarters in the United States employed only three staff members to work on its international programs; their work consisted of introducing new missionaries to their work abroad and publishing a newsletter.

In contrast, Adventists have annual reports going back to 1899, including information and statistics on membership, staff, new members, old members, and baptisms, as well as numbers of schools, hospital, clinics, churches, and money donated to the church. The Adventist organizational model has helped especially in achieving impressive international growth. By the 1920s, an equal number of Adventists existed outside as inside the United States. By the year 2000, the number of those outside the United States had grown to more than ten times the number inside, reaching a total of 17 million members worldwide, compared to 600,000 members worldwide for the Pentecostal Church of God. The world headquarters of the Adventists in Silver Spring, Maryland, employ 250 people who supervise the work of the 13 district offices covering the world.[8]

I visited the Inter-American district office in Miami, where I encountered 60 well-trained analysts examining statistical information from a multitude of countries in Mesoamerica, the Caribbean, and northern South America. Their job was to assess programs and potential problems with regard to work, staffing, finances, and membership. Staff members with language abilities suited to a particular country developed specialized programs for youth, married couples, the elderly, and other types of outreach efforts.

Adventist Practice Throughout Belize

The Adventist church in Belize has grown steadily from the 1960s to the present, and accounts for 10 percent of the total population of the country. Consistent with its centralized corporate model, the church owns a sizable building housing its headquarters in Belize City. Its entrance is gated, leading to a reception area, a small library, and offices for a staff of nine, including the receptionist who escorted me upstairs to the director's office. The director explained their in-country organization and procedures. Cayo was divided into four zones, each assigned at least ten college-educated pastors at any given time. Annual events held throughout the calendar year included Elders' Day and ten days dedicated to conducting evangelistic campaigns. I met with the youth director who was eager to tell me that the goal for his program was to teach young people about essential virtues and how to uphold them, specifically including discipline, self-respect, and self-esteem. The national organization supervised 85 churches altogether.

Adventists in Bullet Tree Falls

In 1972, Raymond Mundall, a physician, and his wife Evelyn, an educator, brought the Adventist religion to Bullet Tree Falls, following Ellen White's ideals of spreading health and education as well as the faith. Their son John told me that they were inspired by the Evangelical philosophy expressed in the writings of Jesus's disciple Matthew, who encouraged "going forth to teach among nations." The Mundalls chose the location for their missionary work after the Inter-American Division of their church informed them that the need was greatest in Belize. In contrast, the Pentecostal Parnell brothers had no bureaucracy to guide them, finding their way to Bullet Tree Falls through vision and inspiration.[9]

Raymond Mundall closed his clinical practice in Arizona in 1972, loaded four trucks with furniture from the clinic, along with his personal possessions, and headed south to set up shop in Santa Elena, Belize, which is the twin town bordering San Ignacio. As a practitioner holding a medical degree from Loma Linda Medical College, he started a local clinic that would steadily grow to become the Loma Luz Adventist Hospital. In 2012, it had 20 in-patient beds, three cribs for infants, a unit for dialysis, and a unit for CAT scans. In a period of four decades it became the primary hospital in Cayo, not only providing care for the local population, but also for patients from all over Belize who were attracted by its reputation. The hospital also provided an important place of employment for Adventist villagers, many from Bullet Tree Falls, whom the hospital paid to be grounds-keepers and maintenance workers.[10]

The Loma Luz Hospital advertises itself as a haven for Christian healing, offering spiritual guidance and providing all patients with a gift of the Bible. It serves as a major mechanism for recruiting new members into the Adventist faith. Their hospital Website echoes White's aspiration for the hospital to be a royal road to spiritual understanding. The site is explicit: "Patients find spiritual healing as well as physical healing, and many have decided to surrender their lives to Jesus after coming to La Loma Luz." Images of the healing role of Jesus are displayed everywhere in the hospital. Just inside its front doors, I observed two pictures with similar content in the hospital lobby, each one depicting a patient, the patient's family, and the doctor with Jesus standing at the doctor's side, two key collaborators in any healing that would take place.

The Mundalls' influence in Bullet Tree Falls was responsible for establishing two churches, one on each side of the river, two elementary schools in Benque, and a high school and elementary school in Santa Elena.

Villagers Learn to Read

I spoke on the phone with 90-year-old Evelyn Mundall in 2012 and discovered that she was living in Vancouver, Canada with her second husband, also an Adventist leader. She told me that her real work in Belize had started in 1973, when she made weekly Sabbath visits to Bullet Tree Falls to hold Bible Study for a group of five young men and women. Having already become acquainted with several villagers who worked as groundskeepers at the hospital, she was already integrated into a network of villagers who might be inclined to join her study group. The five initial members of this group became the core of Adventist life in Bullet Tree Falls, continuing strong for 40 years up to the time of my fieldwork. Evelyn reveled in telling me the story of the group's success. In their first study session, she found that they could hardly read, a deficit that was to quickly change, "because of the presence of the Lord." Ten minutes after our conversation ended, she called me back, determined to make sure I got it just right, carefully choosing her words: "They were preaching the word of the Lord with power; this was God's miracle."

A Distinguished Church Leader

Carl Marcos, an original member of the study group, went on to become a leader in the rapidly growing church. Approaching 60 years of age when we met, still very strong and vigorous, Carl would get up early every morning to work in his *milpa*, persevering through the day under the blazing sun, while still having plenty of energy left over to attend evening church meetings. He devoted additional time to performing social service work for the church, much of it reaching out to villagers oppressed by poverty, or to those suffering from alcoholism or spousal abuse.

Carl expressed his faith in the letter-writing or "epistolary" tradition of Jesus's disciples, who composed persuasive solicitations intended for the edification of non-believers. These early letters later found their way into the Bible, constituting a significant portion of the New Testament. According to a story well known in the community, Carl wrote a letter making a powerful argument to urge his four brothers to leave their dissolute life and convert to the Adventist faith. The letter had the desired effect and more, as his brothers also became leaders in the church. Carl was an indefatigable evangelist, one year making 41 converts, an achievement recognized by the National Adventist organization in Belize, which then invited him to regional gathering in Panama to be honored as a distinguished lay representative of the faith.

Worshippers in Church

I took careful notes on one particular Sabbath, observing as families entered the relatively large church sanctuary which held about 20 pews, ten on each side of a middle aisle, providing enough seating for about 200 worshippers. Sounding as if it came from mainstream American Protestant tradition, the music consisted of quiet nineteenth-century ballads sung in Spanish mostly translated from English, with measured and lyrical praise of Jesus. I heard no cumbia or Norteño music here, nothing emotionally charged or sexually arousing.

The orderly and low-key music matched the demeanor and clothes of the church-goers. Worshippers looked traditional and conventional in the American standard. Men wore starched shirts, jackets, and ties. Women had an unadorned style that included pressed blouses and skirts, long well-groomed hair, and no distracting feminine ornamentation, such as earrings, rings, bracelets, or necklaces. Families moved in unison, repositioning themselves in the pews according to the pastor's instructions to stand, sit, or kneel down. Worshippers were all on the same page, whether following along in the hymnal or listening to the speakers. None showed any signs of being struck by the Holy Spirit as in Pentecostal services where I had seen worshippers dancing in place, shouting praises, or locking arms to hold each other up.

The routine warm-up for the service was to sing three songs from the Adventist hymnal, a 703-page book, after which worshippers broke out into their own special song, proclaiming to anyone and everyone that the Holy Spirit was their guide for living their lives in the present (again, no replay of an biblical ecstasy). They regarded the Holy Spirit as a force to bring tranquility, fellowship, and spiritual awareness, as expressed in song:

The Holy Spirit won't leave.

The Holy Spirit is here to console, liberate, and guide.

With the Holy Spirit there's peace.

In the Holy Spirit there's love.

The White Cloth Metaphor

This service I attended was organized by Carl Marcos, who proudly brought forward his eldest daughter, Alicia Marcos, a 33-year-old schoolteacher, who told a story about cleaning a dirty white cloth. The story was a metaphor for purifying oneself and getting rid of sin, analogous to removing dirt from the cloth. Alicia posed a question to the congregation about how we should get rid of stubborn stains. Pausing a moment for reflection, she reasoned that ordinary cleansers were not sufficient to accomplish the task; the stubborn stains needed treatment with Clorox, similar to the heavy action of real faith. Then she reflected on the need to get rid of sins that can spoil one's character and relationship with Jesus.

After "setting the stage" with her story, Alicia introduced her brother, a singer in the crooner tradition of Latin America. He was exceptionally well dressed in a suit and tie, appearing to be perfectly handsome and clean-cut, like one of the models pictured in many American church publications, with no visible flaws. Calling upon the purifying agent (the Holy Spirit) to give him strength to perform the cleansing work of the church, he expressed his faith in song while addressing the Lord.

Change me, Holy Spirit, fill me, and cover me

With the Blood of Jesus, I want to be the one who is newly cleansed.

Then he rejoiced in the imminent arrival of the Holy Spirit: "Come, Holy Spirit; fill my soul, fill my soul," stretching out the words "Holy" and "Spirit." After Alicia thanked him, she reminded us that the Holy Spirit is always in reserve, a well from which we can draw to achieve purity. Returning to the metaphor of the cloth, she pointed out the necessity of drying it after it had been cleaned. "The sun's warmth will do the job," she said. "The Holy Spirit provides the sun's heat."

Praising Education

Carl Marcos gave the sermon, picking up on Ellen White's dedication to the social mission of education to imbue people with faith. Marcus focused his remarks on a young man in Africa named Oliver who was so rebellious that neither his parents nor his schoolteachers knew what to do with him. One day a colporteur, selling religious books, sold Oliver's mother one of Ellen White's texts, *The Great Controversy*, which Oliver picked up and read, prompting him to change his life. He began to honor the Sabbath and underwent baptism in the Adventist church, all to the amazement of his family, friends, and schoolteachers. This simple story emphasizes three key features of the Adventist faith: the power of the colporteur, the ability of religious conversion to rescue one from the depths of desperation, and the worldwide reach of the faith.

Alicia reinforced the Adventist educational message. She followed up Oliver's story by praising education as key in the Adventist miracle of change. She returned to a point made in her father's sermon about education by bringing our attention back to the clean-cloth metaphor. Miracles happen, she concluded, if we remain supported by education, hanging our thoughts high, preventing clean cloth from falling in the mud. At this stage the service had been ongoing for 75 minutes, when Carl Marcos announced that school was in session, and members of the congregation clustered into four groups occupying the four corners of the sanctuary to report to each other what they had learned from their daily Bible study. After school, everyone reassembled to participate in the remainder of the service. (See Figure 5.4 Adventist Religious School.)

Evidence for the Advent

Afterwards, the scholarly Adventist tradition came to life in the village Adventist church. Carl introduced his nephew, Esteban Marcos, a young Biblical scholar in his twenties, appearing a bit scruffy for an Adventist, more like a nerdy graduate

Figure 5.4 Adventist religious school.

student, stressed out from burning the midnight oil. Relying on his years of study, he gave a virtuoso demonstration of Biblical knowledge to illustrate how soon we are to experience the "Advent" or second coming. He pointed out signs in the contemporary world as evidence that the end of time was near, specifically referring to the worldwide depression of 2008 and ongoing violent conflicts in the Middle East. He singled out passages from the books of John, Kings 1 and 2, Jeremiah, and Matthew to further support his argument. Everyone then sang the final hymn, "Trust and Obey," which was about finding comfort in the knowledge that all would be well for those who embrace the Adventist faith. At the end of the service families filed out of the church, addressing other churchgoers with their usual salutation, "Happy Saturday."

Stories of Miracles: Affirming the Spiritual Powers of Adventists

Adventists held revival meetings twice per year over a period of one week on each occasion. At one of these events in 2011, I listened to their stories about miracles that proved God's power and the importance of having faith in God. Stories about Biblical miracles are part of the broader tradition of Christian testimony about the greatness of Jesus. Listeners suspend everyday rational thought and experience no doubts when they consider that Jesus cleansed the lepers, walked on water, made the blind see, and netted extraordinary catches of fish. Like other Christians, Adventists regard the elimination of disbelief as the sign of real faith. Extrapolating on this theme, the Adventists expanded their repertoire to include stories about relatively recent miracles that have occurred in their lifetimes and are no less extraordinary than the ones performed by Jesus.

Royal, the chaplain at the Loma Luz Hospital, was a key figure in the village revival meeting. He was a dramatic speaker whose voice reached a crescendo in the tenor range when he spoke of God's greatness, and descended into deep, bass tones when he described his own physical trials and rediscovery of God. His tales were so vigorous they erased any traces of skepticism that might be lodged in worshippers' minds.

In church, one would not question the power of God any more than one would doubt the Bible's accounts of Jesus's miracles. On the first night of the revival, Royal told us about being discharged from the hospital after having his foot amputated. He asked a woman at the checkout desk about the cost of the surgery and the prosthetic foot the doctors had provided for him. The woman answered that there would be no cost at all for either one.

I asked, "What is the value of the foot?"

"Seven thousand U.S. dollars," she said.

"And the cost?" I asked.

"None," she said. There was no charge.

Then he met a manufacturer who invited him to visit a workshop in the United States where he promised to give Royal an even better foot. All Royal had to do was to pay for the trip.

But, I didn't have money to pay for a ticket, and a family member, who heard about my problem, bought me the ticket. Then the man who made the foot for me gave me another and I have another at home.

Royal was on a roll in telling the story of his three prosthetic feet and his ticket to travel to the United States. Marveling to us about the unceasing flow of benefits coming his way, he told us about another bonanza that came in a phone call:

"Do you want a new car?" I was asked. Of course I wanted a new car. "How much?" I asked. I was told it was BZ $6,000. "No problem," I was told. "Go to the bank and it will be there."

Then he continued to embellish his account.

Someone put up a partition in my home worth BZ $2,000. And Brother Saguro put up all the doors in my house and installed a kitchen. He has not charged me.

At last came his punch line: "So I tell you today, if you have Jesus Christ and you seek him first, he will provide for you."

ON THE SECOND NIGHT   Royal told us more about his hospital experience. Problems occurred in his treatment that prevented him from swallowing, and he did not "taste water for about two to three weeks." Nurses tried to rehydrate his body by inserting an intravenous tube in his veins, causing them to burst because he was so dehydrated. After two to three weeks of suffering in this condition and reaching the cusp of death, he "talked to God" and "he healed me." He likened himself to the fabulously rich and fatally ill Hezekiah, the King of Judah, mentioned in the Hebrew Bible. Even with his great wealth and power, Hezekiah was destined to die from his illness because he lacked faith. Once he proved himself a true believer, the Lord gave him 15 more years to live.

The message on the first night was modern in its orientation toward materialism, promising that it is possible to live the good life surrounded by material benefits if one is faithful. On the second night, we learned that material benefits are never enough; health and life itself must come from faith to recover from illness.

My Personal Reactions

I might have considered Royal's implausible stories to be wild fabrications if I had heard them in another setting, but his delivery was so high-powered that I got caught up in sharing his enthusiasm. I was very far from being able to take issue with anything he said, not a very consistent response from this cautious academic. Only later when I read the transcript of his presentation did I realize how much I was drawn into the story. Royal knew all about what it takes to generate excitement, and suspend any disbelief. We were all enticed to give ourselves over to faith in God.

More Guidance from Outside the Church

Royal's boss, Grant McPherson, director of the Loma Luz Hospital, had his own story that he would tell to anyone willing to listen. He even printed it for distribution under the title "Between Here and Now," and he handed out free copies to anyone interested. The story goes as follows: a nurse at the front desk of the hospital made call to McPherson to inform him that the hospital's electrocardiograph (EKG) machine was broken. McPherson advised her that they should pray to solve the problem. While they were praying, a second call came to McPherson from the same nurse to report that a physician vacationing in Belize had just arrived from Boston and placed an EKG machine on her desk. The visiting doctor could not explain why he brought the machine, and had no idea why he stopped into his Boston office that morning before boarding the plane. As he entered the office, he noticed that it was dark except for a mysterious source of light shining on an EKG machine. Instinctively he picked up the machine, and the light went out right away. Assuming the light to be a sign that he must take along the machine, he packed it into his travel bag. After arriving in Belize, he felt as if he were on "automatic pilot," controlled by an unexplained external force. He rented a car and drove up the Western Highway, not knowing anything about his destination or why he was going there. Upon arriving in Santa Elena, he set his eyes on Loma Luz Hospital for the first time, and recognized it because the hospital had appeared to him in a dream the night before. He entered the hospital, still not being able to explain his actions, and dropped off the EKG machine on the nurse's desk. The traveling physician remained befuddled about his own behavior and never understood the spiritual force behind it; he was not a believer and not at all disposed to follow

Christ, but could be unknowingly used by Christ at least according to McPherson. For McPherson, the reason for the physician's actions were clear—the hand of God was moving the physician and the machine toward the hospital in Santa Elena.

NARRATIVES AS MECHANISMS FOR CHANGE

Often-heard stories shape people's identity, provide them with readily accessible moral lessons, and guide them in how to live their lives. The familiar story of Horatio Alger is a classic tale casting America as the land of boundless opportunity, and Americans as rugged individuals capable of overcoming hardship and capitalizing on that opportunity through diligence and clean living. The biblical story of David tells how a much smaller and younger man, presumably overmatched in strength and agility, relied on his faith, courage, and skill with an underrated weapon to fell a giant enemy warrior. Many Christians and Jews, and even some secularists, identify with David, the underdog with the odds stacked against him seeking to overcome a hostile world. Like David, they believe they have the moral strength and cleverness to prevail. The humanities and social sciences today recognize the importance of narratives as key mechanisms in any culture to transmit, share, and reinforce ideas about common identity, interpretation of the world around us, and how to behave appropriately. Evangelical missionaries changed the culture of Bullet Tree Falls; they brought a constellation of cultural knowledge new to villagers. Their schemas of thought challenged listeners to respond and often made them fearful and desirous of personal change.

Cognitive anthropologist Roy D'Andrade has observed how words, stories, and artifacts can serve as vehicles to shape human cognition and behavior (1995: xiv). In this chapter, I have followed his lead in uncovering the power of narratives— Bible stories and sacred testimonies—to understand how Evangelicals were able to bring about profound changes in Bullet Tree Falls.[11]

Narratives of Pentecostals and Adventists contain three essential ingredients that make them effective—defining the social identity of believers; conveying a belief that the world will be better; relating that we will be better prepared for Jesus if we just follow his commandments; and finally, a presentation of a moral code by which the young and families need to live in order to achieve contentment on earth and everlasting life beyond one's time on earth. Evangelicals answered the fundamental questions of life: Who are we? Where are we? What are we supposed to be doing here? The fundamental questions are not confined to Evangelicals; they express a universal need. Ted Downing (1996) of the University of Arizona discovered the importance of these three questions as experienced by populations of involuntarily displaced people, most often removed and resettled away from their ancestral lands to make way for development. He found that they typically experience a debilitating loss of collective identity, confusion about where they really belong in both a spatial and temporal sense, as well as loss of a contemporary religious ritual sense.

In Bullet Tree Falls, we see how imported religion provided new answers to these fundamental questions. Religious conversion enabled people to reject old narratives, old identities, and seemingly outmoded ideas about the right way to live. Historic solutions to daily problems no longer worked in a satisfactory manner. New narratives presented them with compelling solutions to problems that pose a real existential threat such as alcohol abuse, wasteful spending of money, disintegrating family life, illness, physical disability, educational deprivation, ethnic conflict, or even the breakdown of instruments, (like the EKG machine) in a technological age. It was not feasible for many villagers in Bullet Tree Falls to continue to depend on spirit protectors or look forward to the next festival as a major reward in life. Religious converts among Bullet Tree Falls residents had replacements for historic narratives to help in adapting to a changing world and the difficulties it presented, whereas in Downing's case these narratives were regrettably absent.

In their narratives Evangelicals also provided comforting answers for people suffering from the universal human anxiety about what happens after death. Villagers who became believers would never quite know if they got their final reward, because no one could come back from the dead to complain. In this sense Evangelicals are insulated from the kind of failed outcomes and ultimate disappointments that tend to subvert community interventions intended to bring about economic change.

The narratives of Evangelicals, exported from America, motivated people to give up Catholicism and produced comprehensive transformations, conveying to new believers the idea that they were among the "saved," committed to following Jesus and living an entirely different life free of alcohol and sin. Leaving non-believers completely on the outside, the narratives acted like scalpels making incisions in the social body, producing schisms even among family members, while at the same time quickly and effectively introducing social change and cohesion in church communities. As a result of these Evangelical incursions, the community of Bullet Tree Falls became fragmented along religious lines but people found new religious groups which provided affiliation and an orientation to life.

If a narrative is to be more than a cold, stern morality tale or a stale recitation of the need for progress, it must be pleasurable to read or hear. The narratives of Pentecostals are deeply sentimental, spiritual, even psychedelic or mind-expanding, while those of the Adventists are dramatic portrayals that elicit wonder, respect, and admiration. In both cases, the delivery of the story gratifies the listener, providing the key to open the schemas and formulae that whisk away uncertainty about the future and provide a continuing sense of security. The Parnells supercharged their message with theatrical embellishments, including music, movies, and a light show, and induced a state of ecstasy among worshippers. The Mundalls added credibility and sustainability to their message by building and managing an impressive hospital. Local church leaders, who were successors to the Mundalls, tantalized listeners' imaginations with tales beyond the limits of ordinary experience. In both types of Evangelical faith, Pentecostal and Social Gospel Evangelicals, narratives provided a core of gripping entertainment that captured the commitment and loyalty of believers.

Both Pentecostals and Adventists owe their success at least partly to a key ingredient of effective communication across geographical and cultural boundaries—they have already gotten their story straight well in advance of undertaking their mission, and they always show up well prepared, not settling for an unpredictable experiment in ad hoc persuasion. They knew what to say, having mastered all elements of the lead story of salvation, along with a clear depiction of what comes in the afterlife and minor stories about how to face everyday situations and challenges. Their stories always find a life of their own; not simply tales told, heard, and forgotten, they become infectious and acquire proven durability, enabling believers to be confident in offering the same stories to a wider humanity. In the case of the Pentecostals the strength of the message derives from the characteristics of the American frontier; in the case of the Adventists, it derives from nineteenth-century Protestant themes of civic-mindedness, health, and literacy. The global transmission of their messages was just a matter of personal delivery of narratives worked out well in advance and integrated into the lives of missionaries. Very capable leaders orchestrated the narrative routines I witnessed in Bullet Tree Falls. Their confidence meant that conversions were a foregone conclusion. They had their act together.

Finally, the success of Evangelical missionaries in Bullet Tree Falls was due to a long-term presence and immersion in the local community, while exhibiting a clear and steady purpose. They accomplished their conversions in person-to-person transactions that offered clear benefits in exchange for commitment and loyalty. Their endeavors and those of their successors were not interrupted by uneven flows of international support or undermined by policies in agency or government offices far removed from the realities of local village culture. By the time the missionaries had done their work, they were able to leave behind a nucleus of followers capable of continuing to bring in new converts and strengthen the community of believers.

6/Rethinking Globalization and Change

I started my research focusing on the El Pilar project and on Anabel Ford as the change agent bringing cultural influences from afar. However, I could not avoid noticing other influences from across the globe that had reshaped the lives of villagers in Bullet Tree Falls—in particular the Rastafarians, the cooperative movement, and the Evangelical missionaries, thus arousing my curiosity about the broader subject of globalization and how its manifestations might affect a community in a variety of ways. Bullet Tree Falls offered a diverse and inviting laboratory of change, as well as a welcoming community where I found few barriers to conducting my inquiry, at least in part because it had no political elites ensconced in a civil-religious hierarchy who might resist change as a means to hold onto their status. Now at the end of the book I want to reflect on what I have learned and characterize globalization as a process—how it happens, and what mechanisms of change work or do not work, and how we all might be involved in steering the process of global change.

LESSONS FROM BULLET TREE FALLS

Globalization Creates Diversity and Community Fragmentation   Each of the four major influences (described in Chapters 2–5) had a distinctive impact on the community creating a promise of a positive future but also divisiveness. Ford's project to establish a new tourist enterprise based on Maya cultural legacy included a portion of the village attracted by her promises, but the government's actions in implementing the project soon created a bitter divide between Ford and villagers who were required to cope with the loss of farmland. Creoles living in their own enclave became Rastafarians pursuing a distinctive livelihood shaped by attitudes and styles largely imported from Jamaica. The cooperative movement for a while stood out as a distinctive subculture, as its organizational principles were antagonistic to traditional cultural values. Evangelical missionaries introduced a set of beliefs, attitudes, and behaviors that became dominant among a large segment of the Maya-Mestizo population, spiritually and socially separating them from a Catholic way of life that had once prevailed without challenge. Even the Evangelical population showed substantial diversity, divided between Pentecostals and Social Gospel Evangelicals, the latter further divided into separate sects—Adventists,

Mormons, and Jehovah's Witnesses. Each Evangelical group hunkered down in its own enclave, self-confident with its own spiritual orientation. Globalization was not a simple matter of one single effect washing over an entire community to produce a uniform set of changes; instead the effects were multiple and varied, causing different types of changes in different parts of the community.

The speed of globalization varies according to periods of time defined by particular economic, political, and social conditions. Globalization comes in surges, accelerating and decelerating, not necessarily proceeding at a steady rate. Historically, it was clear that globalization sped up in Bullet Tree Falls when Belize was opening to the outside world in the period leading up to and just after independence in 1981. At this time, agents of change from abroad seized the opportunity to shape the future of Belize and Bullet Tree Falls—sometimes with altruistic purposes, sometimes with the objective of stimulating economic progress to create opportunity for themselves or business partners, and sometimes intending to make their mark on the world and become famous. The anthropological tradition recognizes that communities sometimes become more open to the outside world and then close off, only to open again, years or decades later. The emerging diverse culture in Bullet Tree Falls was an outcome of shedding the protective shield of a colonial power, Great Britain, and a conscious effort on the part of the government to develop the country with open-door policies, not merely allowing, but deliberately encouraging foreign influence.

Globalization produces lasting impacts, even if the imported project or program is short-lived. Agricultural cooperatives that had started with fanfare 30 years ago before I came to Bullet Tree Falls mostly disappeared after less than a decade. While I was working in the village, agricultural cooperatives were a minor issue, a distant memory. At first, I seriously questioned the importance of gathering information about projects that had mostly melted away. Soon I found that I could not discount the lasting effects of collective memory and deep feelings associated with the experience of change and interaction with change agents. When a program runs out of steam and no longer has an obvious impact, its effects may still be strong, as I found to be true of the cooperative movement. Villagers' disappointing experiences and subsequent cynicism about cooperatives convinced them of their inability to get along with each other in a collective enterprise, and it fostered the notion that they were somehow incapable of accepting and benefiting from international assistance programs.

Villagers' experiences with Ford's initiative and enthusiasm led to the same kind of distrust and cynicism about foreign intervention that was also evident in the cooperative movement. However, in the case of Ford, there were favorable outcomes that could lend themselves to some level of economic advancement. Villagers did develop a new consciousness about their ability to profit from the commercial value of ethnicity as a commodity. Young people gained appreciation for nature and the possibilities it might hold in the future for attracting tourists.

The outcomes of global initiatives are affected by goals, cultural context, and preparedness at the source of change.   Even before new beliefs and practices make their journey across the globe to places like Bullet Tree Falls, planning and preparation at the source of change shape strategies and eventual outcomes. The Rastafarian way smoothly gained a foothold in Belize and Bullet Tree Falls at least partly because Bob Marley and Chris Blackwell, in their celebration of cultural and racial hybridity, latched onto universally appealing themes of peace, love, and oneness, echoing the liberalization of attitudes that became part of popular culture in the Western world of the 1960s and subsequent decades. By bringing in Wayne Perkins, the good old boy, to play guitar on his recordings, Marley seamlessly crossed international boundaries with his message. From his experience in Caye Caulker, Henry Coleman was able to effectively transmit Rastafarian beliefs because he already understood their appeal and the process of change that would take place in Bullet Tree Falls.

Pentecostal missionaries had formulated their stories and emotionally charged rituals of conversion in Oklahoma and tested them in cross-cultural settings with Spanish and Indian populations. Ernest Parnell's children learned the routines from him, and in the 1970s, they left well equipped with prior experience to spread their faith in Belize. The brilliant success of the Adventist Mundalls was founded on 150 years of steady church growth and its enormous commitment to work outside the country. The fact that 90 percent of Adventist church members reside outside the United States is testimony to the universal efficacy of the methods they employed. Adventist missionaries were well prepared not only with stories of the second coming, but also with the capability to deliver highly effective programs of health care and education.

Exhibiting considerable passion, but less preparedness for being a change agent, Ford was enthusiastic about spreading the secular gospel of conservation and showcasing the genius of the ancient Maya. Funding agencies and Belizean political leaders enabled Ford's project to begin; they embraced her progressive American values—conservation of nature, respect for indigenous people and their ancient wisdom, and encouraging community participation. These values and practices came from her own culture and were untested when she transported them across international boundaries.

The export of cooperatives by Canadians and others was like sending detailed instructions on how to run a complex machine when the recipients were not sufficiently or experienced to make sense of them. The routines of cooperative development in diverse cultural settings are elaborate and involve delicate questions about management of interpersonal relations, the apportionment of land and natural resources, working together, accepting leadership, and finding a market for the product. Plans for establishing cooperatives in Belize seemed reasonable, even straightforward, in offices in Ottawa and Nova Scotia, following successes throughout the twentieth century experienced by the cooperative movement in Canada. Similarly, in the European Union boardrooms of Brussels, cooperatives may have seemed to be a logical and fruitful way to advance global commerce. However, what seemed logical and simple in design turned out to be a prescription for problems, as villages were completely unaccustomed to institutions that required mutual cooperation, leadership from within, and trust when a few speak and act for the whole group.

Canadian funders made an effort to dispatch specialists to assist in-country NGOs in their role as overseers of cooperatives, but failed to bring them closer to understanding the actual functioning of the cooperatives. The public relations goals of funders took precedence over correcting operational problems. In the last phase of the cooperative movement, ideologically motivated funders imagined that the force of private enterprise was still untapped. By creating a cadre of technical specialists through the form of a cooperative, the village would prosper through entrepreneurship and capitalism. Bullet Tree Falls would, as well as elsewhere, benefit from what is often called the magic of the market place. However, their plans fell flat because economic development needs continual personal involvement to promote desired practices rather than promulgation of an ideology agreeable to donor sentiments.

Globalization does not necessarily proceed in a straight line.   The idea of globalization seems to imply changes that are durable and set an unwavering course for the future. Two of our four cases of globalization do not meet this expectation, taking twists and turns that might not have been expected. Rastafarianism in Bullet Tree Falls started with the transmission of messages about African pride, dignity, and social harmony, but it wound up stroking the vanities of Rastafarian men, who took advantage of new opportunities in romance tourism and pursued their own interests as members of a self-appointed welcoming committee to profit from North Americans and Europeans who sought to experience a tropical paradise. Gentrification of the community as a result of romance tourism was an equally unexpected twist of fate, when new property owners from North America and Europe moved in and established residences.

The cultural heritage movement also went in an unexpected direction when the El Pilar project fell short as a tourist destination. As the project unfolded, it actually reinforced the impression among villagers that outside forces could be malevolent and given to unfairly exploit them. Villagers eventually broke away to pursue their own projects treating their ethnic heritage as a commodity. The future may hold yet another twist of fate if young people educated abroad and appreciative of their natural and cultural heritage begin to promote their own ecotourism initiatives.

Globalization can induce radical change in cultural and personal identity.   In the context of globalization, dramatic changes often occur when people begin to view themselves differently and adopt a completely different purpose in life. They acquire new mental schemas about who they are, and how they should live.

In Bullet Tree Falls successful interventions by agents of change were typically predicated upon a radical identity makeover. Rastafarians and Evangelicals felt rescued from a previous outlook that deprived them of joy in their everyday lives and offered them little hope for the future. In embracing Haile Selassie and his messengers, Bob Marley and Henry Coleman, the Creole villagers had gained a new sense of pride in being of African origin, embracing the Rastafarian doctrine that the messiah had already arrived on earth for a second time, meaning that the possibilities for living in paradise were close at hand. With soaring self-esteem they internalized the Rastafarian values of social harmony and love and also exploited a sexually appealing identity to prosper from tourism.

They underwent a sudden and overwhelming emotional experience. They had an immediate and comprehensive identity change arising from the realization that they had joined an exclusive group of believers that God had saved them from a life of sin and an eventual eternity in Hell. The rewards of reconnecting with others in their homes and the continuing emotional support provided by the church made it worthwhile to abandon drinking binges, profligate spending habits, and irregular work patterns. Having experienced the heights of identity transformation, they remained steadily and happily on the side of Jesus, enjoying their new lease on this life while maintaining greater hope for the next life.

The importance of personal identity was not lost on the architects of change in cultural heritage tourism. Ford knew that it was important for the success of her project for villagers to embrace their Maya identity and exhibit pride in ancient Maya architectural achievements, folk art, and conservation strategies. For a while, her vision of establishing a Maya environmental display for tourists captured the imagination of her paid employees. However, villagers never adopted a nativistic stance. Many factors got in the way: lack of cultural awareness in managing the project, the absence of ticket sales and steady revenue, and the ambivalent responses of Belizeans who had positions of power in government. None of Ford's followers underwent this identity transformation.

The cooperative movement sought to redefine the social relations involved in village economic life, changing farmers from individual to collective producers. The plans ignored the fact that farmers preferred wholly self-controlled work lives. They were proud of their self-reliance and inclined to be competitive in showing off their farming abilities and providing for their families. Agents working for the cooperative movement tried hard to stimulate collective spirit and mutual trust through efforts such as staging Solidarity Concerts and holding experimental training sessions in nearby San Miguel, but the effects were short-lived. Farmers saw no advantages and many uncertainties in changing the way they pursued their livelihood.

Multiple theoretical positions enhance the description and analysis of globalization.   Before I began my project in Bullet Tree Falls, reviewers who read my proposal for research funding cautioned me about what they perceived as the "complexity" of my study and warned that adopting multiple theoretical perspectives might make fieldwork both difficult and time consuming. They were right—it was difficult and time consuming to move from intervention to intervention, going back and forth between several sets of actors. I had to search out and assemble four different sets of background information from many scattered sources and travel to distant places to hunt down and interview a wide range of people who designed and implemented global initiatives. Despite the demanding nature of this research, the use of different theoretical perspectives (in Chapters 2–5) put me in a position to gain a rich harvest of information and a more profound understanding of the processes and impacts of globalization.

Theory in cultural anthropology is not like theory in physics, which is concerned with establishing an ironclad set of rules that govern the behavior of solids, liquids, gases, etc. Instead, it is closer to a metaphor or an ideal type representing how the world might work. My choice of theory to support my analysis came from examining my findings as I went along; in other words, the information I gathered showed me the way to theory. The defining features of the chosen metaphor or an ideal type then helped to determine what was important to emphasize later in writing my descriptions and analyses. My method was inductive and iterative, with ideas arising from and tested by experience.

In my study of Anabel Ford and cultural heritage tourism, I drew from Eric Wolf's ideas about patron–client relations. In this case I showed how Ford seemed to fall short by not carrying out culturally defined responsibilities to her followers. In my study of Creoles and Rastafarians, I needed to draw upon a broader framework for understanding thoughts and actions, finding utility in Arjun Appadurai's theory about "scapes," a term he uses to describe how ideas, habits of thought, symbols, and cultural practices spread around the globe. Appadurai's emphasis on ideoscapes and mediascapes guided my inquiry. First, the ideoscapes of Garvey and Hyde praising Black power instilled pride in the Creole population. Then mediascapes encouraging social harmony and an inclusive lifestyle arrived in the lyrics of Bob Marley's reggae songs and were similarly conveyed in person by Henry Coleman. When I began observing the workings of cooperatives, Benedict Anderson's book *Imagined Communities: Reflections on the Origin and Spread of Nationalism* (2006) came to mind. I took note of incompatibilities in a dual framework of perceptions—the architects of the cooperative movement imagined that they could remake social relations to respond to the imperative of economic development, and they ran into resistance from villagers who had their own way of organizing their relationships and activities. As I studied the Evangelicals, I was struck by the way narratives etched mental maps in people's minds to guide them on a different path and reinforce new beliefs and moral teachings. The power of the narrative to change people can be dramatic, sudden, and durable over time.

I realize that any single theoretical orientation might be applicable at least to some degree to more than one situation. For example, Henry Coleman's relations with village Creoles might be captured in the motivational power of shared narratives, and the workings of cooperatives might be described in terms of patron and client exchanges. In the same vein, we might think of Ford's admonitions as ideoscapes emanating from progressive American culture alternative to describing patron-client relations and apply the concept of the imagined community to the designs carried out by Evangelical missionaries. However, certain theoretical approaches, more than others, led me to the heart of the matter in each case. Consequently, I benefitted from the flexibility to select theoretical approaches that most effectively lead to the best understanding of diverse situations and circumstances.

This kind of flexible approach is typical of applied behavioral science, where researchers are comfortable with employing a "transtheoretical model" (Prochaska

2014), formulated from drawing upon multiple theories. Basically, this is a fancy way of saying that we are going to select whatever works to describe, understand, and draw conclusions about our topic of research. Although introducing yet another technical term in anthropology is hardly necessary, I am convinced that studies of globalization and other phenomena with internal variability can benefit from the interpretive flexibility conveyed by the term "transtheoretical."[1]

WHAT WE CAN DO?

The cases examined in this book underscore various steps we should take to enhance efforts to bring about intentional change. The shortcomings of bureaucratically sponsored initiatives and the seemingly spontaneous successes of Rastafarians and Pentecostals provide clues on what we should and should not emulate.

The Role of Applied Anthropologists in Facilitating Change

No question exists about the need for skilled professionals equipped to understand cultural differences and build bridges between change agents and intended recipients of change. Working in the context of a cultural heritage tourism project, an applied anthropologist could have explored responses of the tourists, the attitudes and norms of participants and residents in host communities, as well as the assumptions and values of the change agents. Cooperative organizations have long been a preoccupation for applied anthropology, applied sociologists, institutional economists, and other professionals who are concerned with moving production and marketing away from hierarchical control and corporate business models. In conducting research on a cooperative program, an applied anthropologist could have offered advice to change agents about including cultural analysis in their designs for organization, implementation, and administration, not only regarding village culture, also awareness of their own culture; as it shapes policy, planning, and implementation within the nation-state, development agencies, and funding institutions.

The strategies of Rastafarians in spreading their message about *ganja* and love seem an unlikely source to find clues for carrying out economic development. However, the promotion and marketing tools that made Rastafarianism appealing are also familiar to applied anthropologists, some of whom work in marketing and promotion, seeking to influence culturally diverse consumers to purchase cars, computers, clothes, and other mundane products. As far as I know, Chris Blackwell, Bob Marley's manager, had no training in applied anthropology, but he was keen on marketing and finding hybrid and enticing expressions of reggae that could easily cross cultural boundaries. His promotion of Marley to diverse audiences shows that it is important to have someone at the helm capable of understanding cultural mixes.

Religious organizations involved in sending missionaries overseas are also aware of the importance of culture and sometimes seek advice from applied anthropologists. While being guided around the Inter-American District Office of the

Adventist organization, I met an employee who identified himself as an applied anthropologist specializing in missiology—that is, the strategies of carrying out missionary work in culturally unfamiliar terrain. His task was to spread the Adventist religion and use anthropology to get the job done. On his bookshelves I observed the same texts I frequently assign to anthropology students, along with a series of Adventist publications containing instructions about how to be a missionary among Hindus, Jews, Catholics, and other religious groups. Missionary work was not my calling, definitely not what I chose to do; but I concede that Adventists know how to use the tools of planning, management, and social science.

The Need for Planning to Take into Account the Stages of Intervention

Relatively recently, the word "sustainability" has been added to the criteria for judging the soundness of international development projects. The use of this term demonstrates a commitment not simply to start things off, but to keep them going. Change agents sometimes assume that new programs and projects after being launched with the appropriate amount of fanfare will chug along on their own steam without further intervention. The collapse of some programs and projects in Bullet Tree Falls shows the importance of considering innovative solutions to achieve sustainability to keep the program going.

For analytic purposes, we need to do a thorough preparatory research before the on-the-ground intervention. I suggest that interventions to bring about intentional change can be broken down into three phases: the launch phase, the maintenance phase, and a phase of reproduction and replication. Each phase deserves separate consideration in the planning process. Plans might vary in terms of how to manage each of the three phases. I draw upon examples from Bullet Tree Falls.

Launch The launch or beginning focuses initial attention on an inspiring vision of the future and setting goals that will bring great benefits to participants and their community. Leaders begin to inspire people through the use of motivational speeches, ceremony, music, and the promise of a better life. The launch phase was successful using at least some of these techniques in all four cases of intervention in Bullet Tree Falls, but did not automatically translate into sustainability.

Maintenance The maintenance phase involves monitoring progress and potential barriers to progress to ensure that a program continues at a level of operation equal to its start-up efficiency. The tasks involved in this stage are neither as glamorous nor as entertaining as those in the launch, but they are just as important. The programs promoting cultural heritage tourism and cooperatives were very strong at the start, but later suffered from the neglect of maintenance. Change agents ignored problems, were incapable of dealing with deteriorating interpersonal relations, and could not restore sagging confidence in leaders. Their regimen lacked regular onsite evaluation, current reports of unfolding events, and meaningful counseling provided to local leaders of cooperatives. In contrast, Rastafarian and Evangelical understudies received steady mentoring and support until such point that they were ready to carry on the mission on their own.

Reproduction and Replication In the reproduction and replication phase, the existing program recharges its forward progress and stimulates new initiatives that seek to duplicate its past successes in other settings, either nearby or far away. In this phase at least a few loyal followers must be knowledgeable and skilled enough to carry on and repeat the efforts of their leaders and mentors. Their success will depend on early training and experience given to them in the launch and maintenance phases, not as a sudden afterthought. In regard to cultural heritage tourism and cooperatives, a core group to carry on the program did not emerge because of lack of foresight, low morale, and the ultimate collapse of the programs themselves. From the beginning, Rastafarians and Evangelicals cultivated core groups of followers to pass along their message and mentor new converts.

The Need to become Aware of Core Values

Any intentional intervention to bring about change must respect core values of intended beneficiaries if it is ever going to take hold. Core values function as a social and psychological substrate on which people will evaluate their experience in any new program or project. Lack of attention to existing core values may provoke fierce resistance, all too quickly. The main features of this social and psychological substrate are defined by existential questions such as: Who are we? Where are we? What are we supposed to be doing here? The answers reveal core values that might make or break a project intervention.

In Bullet Tree Falls, the core values of individualism and commitment to one's family were inviolable. Cultural heritage tourism and cooperatives did not progress as intended because core values stood in the way of farmers easily relinquishing their control of cherished farmland and their autonomy as independent decision makers. The violations of core values became especially egregious when material sacrifices made by project participants failed or were slow to yield anticipated benefits.

Success that came to the beekeeper and poultry cooperatives, which were structurally based on rewarding individual production, speaks well for programs that emerge from the heart of a culture and are inherently consistent with core values. Rastafarians and Evangelicals easily gained a foothold because their message rang true to the core values of peace and social harmony acceptable to all refugee families. I do not mean to insinuate that global programs consistent with local core values may not face considerable risks. Merely, I wish to emphasize that those on the outside doing the exporting need to know the local culture, inside and out, and then make the necessary program adjustments to fit the culture. Acquiring cultural knowledge and awareness is a central part of becoming sufficiently prepared.

The Importance of Self-Awareness by Planners

Cultural values, familiar practices, and preparedness of change agents play a critical role in the success or failure on any intentional program of change. Each of the four interventions I have documented was an outcome of cultural context and accepted practices that shaped the design of the intervention at the source and inspiration for change at some globally distant location. Programs of intervention and change are often crafted with the destination that is culturally as well as geographically different and distant. The fate of the program depends on a preparedness to change course and approaches—as might have happened in the cultural tourism venture where the social and ecological agenda did not adapt to Bullet Tree Falls. The Canadians and Europeans promoting cooperatives were disposed to create work in a collective enterprise though they did not change their methods and approaches when running into a highly individualistic community. They continued to act with extreme confidence in their designs and focus on self-promotion, so much so they were inattentive to monitoring and correcting operational flaws. Rastafarians and Evangelicals were equally confident, but knew their own culture and how their beliefs and values might appeal to the people they sought to change. They had learned by experience to immerse themselves in the community, and to proceed progressively, appealing to individuals in spreading their message from one person to another.

The Need for Flexibility and Independence in Managing Change

The work of program leaders needs to be more than a clearly defined list of responsibilities. Reconciling local demands with expectations from the architects of change is no easy task. It entails a freedom of action, independence, and creativity in dealing with these architects of change—unburdened by the misperceptions and rigidity of a remote bureaucracy. The efforts of Rastafarians and Evangelical missionaries were successful in large part because those invested in making change were autonomous spending time in the community and they could continually assess the local situation and act accordingly. All programs need the same capacity to adapt to unforeseen and changing realities.

The Importance of Tangible Pay-offs and Quick Returns

Beyond initial hype and excitement, the payoff for participants' commitment to any program of change must involve financial or material benefits delivered in a timely and predictable manner. If such payoffs are not forthcoming, as happened in cultural heritage tourism and the cooperative movement, then doubts set in, old patterns of suspicion and interpersonal conflict emerge, and rhetoric of leaders about the organization and its underlying principles and values falls on deaf ears. Participants are likely to drop their commitment if they feel that they have been misled by unfulfilled promises.

No agent of change or program can ever be error-free, but passing along dividends to compensate for a personal investment early in the process protects against disappointment and a lapse into dysfunctional behavior. Evangelical converts receive their payoff in two ways—the immediate benefit of a more energized and satisfying lifestyle, and the certain promise of everlasting life. Because the latter is a matter of faith not subject to empirical verification, Evangelical missionaries remain insulated from the harsh need to demonstrate a tangible, long-term payoff. Rastafarians also conferred the immediate benefit of a more satisfying personal image and lifestyle, involving camaraderie and mutual support at first and afterwards the opportunity for long-term, regular dividends derived from romance tourism. Beekeepers and chicken farmers were consistently and quickly rewarded for their efforts.

The Importance of Intangible Accoutrements and Spiritual Elevation

Intangible forms of gratification may constitute motivators equal in importance to material rewards and improvements in lifestyle. For change to be personally compelling it also has to confer social and psychological benefits involving spirituality and emotions, not simply instrumental gain. In using the term "spirituality," I am not limiting its meaning to theistic beliefs, but broadly referring to deeper satisfactions that go beyond the mundane concerns of daily life.

Ceremony and motivational speaking directed toward uplifting people's spirits are important in forging a sense of common purpose and social bonding among participants. In all four cases I have presented, participants initially found energy in opening salvos, along with personal support and encouragement from a more knowledgeable leader. Such encouragements were missing after the first stages of the El Pilar project and internationally funded cooperatives. Long-lasting attention to spiritual and personal needs contributed to successes in the case of Evangelicals, Rastafarians, and the beekeepers and poultry cooperatives. Pentecostal Evangelicals shared the ecstasy of speaking in tongues. Adventists had the solace of their beliefs, support, and rituals, while the Rastafarians elevated spirituality by "getting high with a little help from their friends." Sometimes change agents tend to neglect sentient and spiritually uplifting reinforcements after they think participants are hooked and committed to a project. Agents of change should not forget that people meet their needs and find satisfactions in ways that go far beyond the stated material objectives of any program or project.

CONCLUDING THOUGHTS

As an anthropologist studying globalization, I have attempted to show how we humans try to create new cultural realities through interpersonal transactions that tie together people who otherwise have different histories and live in different parts of the world. In this book we have traced four different kinds of interventions from the United States, Canada, Europe, and Jamaica, each following separate paths to Bullet Tree Falls, and each having different, and sometimes unexpected, outcomes.

All of us are involved in an interconnected global community where interventions involve policies, motivations, strategies, narratives, and ritual trappings that shape our common and separate futures. I hope readers of this book no longer regard globalization merely as a symphony of uncontrollable forces carving a centrally orchestrated path through digital information carried in news, entertainment, and advertising. Nor should we view globalization primarily as a spate of economic and political institutions—from trade agreements to international banks to Starbucks and McDonald's—marching to the beat of neo-liberal economics.

Person-to-person transactions across cultural boundaries, sometimes effective and sometimes not, are at the core of how larger trends will develop in changing people's livelihoods, beliefs, and lifestyle.

Using the cross-cultural perspective of anthropology, I have tried to increase awareness of how ideologies, values, actions, reactions, and transactions across vast geographical expanses have varied effects on real people living in remote locations. However, the task of increasing awareness does not end with the conclusion to this book; it is incumbent on us all to convey, at every opportunity, how those who bankroll, design, and manage intentional change can do better and act with greater compassion and competence toward communities with different cultural traditions. Not confined to geographically distinctive communities, change confronts us everywhere. In our everyday lives we might ask ourselves how we can constructively contribute, either professionally or personally, to understanding and coping with a culturally diverse and rapidly changing world. In a profound sense, we are all agents of change in our own cultures and communities, and I believe that we can prepare ourselves to act responsibly in meeting the inevitable challenges that will come from change that we either initiate or experience ourselves.

Appendix

EXCERPTS OF AN INTERVIEW WITH THE HONOURABLE GEORGE CADLE PRICE

I present excerpts from my interview with George Price, as recorded on June 9, 2011, from 2:00 to 3:30 P.M. It is of potential interest to readers concerned with a number of topics including: Belize as a whole, its colonial history, its establishment as a new nation, and the intertwining politics and the Catholic doctrine of social justice. This interview was most important for establishing the historical context of my study. In his role as leader of the People's United Party for almost a half a century, Price earned a reputation as a statesman with considerable domestic and international stature. He died on September 19, 2011, several months after my interview. I recorded our conversation with his permission. We sat across his desk in a very informal living room scattered with toys for the use of those who filled in as if great-grandchildren. I refer the reader to Figure 4.2, a photo taken during our interview. The transcribed interview included minimal editing to avoid repetition and emphasize highlights.

Catholicism and Colonialism

Gordon: My question is about the architects or social engineers of development and their intended influence in Belize; I want to know what have been most significant influences on Belize in the 1950s, '60s, '70s, and '80s?

Price: Well, it was the colonial system. It had something good in it, but something bad, keeping us backwards; we had to get rid of it. We got rid of the old colonial system to bring in the Christian heritage, the freedom of religion, and freedom of speech.

At one time, in the 1970s when we were trying to get rid of the British colonial system, we sang "God Bless America" at political meetings.

Mr. Gordon: Just to say that you too may become a de-colonialized society from England?

Mr. Price: Yes.

Mr. Gordon: Your Christian heritage has been influential. Tell me about that, please.

Mr. Price: Well, I was a Jesuit trained. I am a Catholic and I am in good standing with my church, not too far from here. I read *The Tablet* (a worldwide Catholic periodical), the church's teachings and of course the big newspapers.

Mr. Gordon: You used to go to mass every day?

Mr. Price: I used to go before I became very sick and was in the hospital.

Mr. Gordon: Could you be specific for me, please, about what aspects of the Catholic teachings were important to you?

Mr. Price: The papal encyclicals were most important, especially those on labor and justice in society. The preamble of the constitution and the whole constitution of Belize draws on the papal encyclicals on matters of labor and justice in society.* They are good guides because they have already done the work. All those hands have done the work. [It was] bright people who did it. The way you write, people will read it. All the papal encyclicals were influential.

Mr. Gordon: Are there any encyclicals you could point me to which would be particularly helpful to my understanding?

Mr. Price: As a basic one, Leo XIII (the encyclical of the *Rerum Novarum*) and Pius XI. I like the modern pope, John Paul II.

I am somewhat of a socialist, drawing on the wisdom of the encyclicals and the Bible, but I don't think I am a communist, although I have studied it. I like the New Testament, the beatitudes, and the account of the blessed mother, Mary, the mother of Christ, and the history of Christ's life.

Mr. Gordon: Do you see Jesus's life as a model for your own life?

Mr. Price: I try to follow him and that's why I went among of people. I used to first go into their kitchen, not to interfere with them. It was an economic study to see what they were eating. If I saw the bones of a bird I knew they were poor.

Mr. Gordon: There have been a number of currents in the Catholic Church over the years, one of them being the Theology of Liberation. How did you see that?

Mr. Price: I would support parts of it. I liked the Nicaraguans, the Jesuit University in Nicaragua and in El Salvador.

Mr. Gordon: Specifically, which part did you support?

Mr. Price: The socialist part.

Mr. Gordon: Which parts did you not support?

Price: The atheist one.

---

*The Preamble to the Constitution, a 393-word document, was published on September 21, 1981. Price's vision is evident throughout the Preamble, specifically his spirituality, sense of social justice, and intention to make economic security the right of all Belizeans.

The Preamble affirms "principles which acknowledge the supremacy of God, faith in human rights and fundamental freedoms ... with which all members of the human family are endowed by their Creator:"

- respect the principles of social justice;
- economic system must result in the material resources of the community being so distributed as to serve the common good and provide adequate means of livelihood for all men, and institutions founded upon respect for moral and spiritual values and the rule of law; and
- the right of the individual to the ownership of private property and the right to operate whether private or by the state; and ensure a just system of social security and welfare.

International Assistance and Development

Mr. Gordon: What were the sources of international assistance?

Mr. Price: International assistance has been important to us in infrastructure, the roads and the bridges and then electricity. We now have hydroelectric power from one of the rivers, and we are moving ahead. We now have television, radio, and communications, so we are right up with the other parts of the world. We know what is going on and we have friends—the United Nations, the various countries giving aid, the United States, also the United Kingdom, Europe, and even the socialist countries. We don't accept all their doctrines. The People's United Party is a socialist party; we are not communist. Our guides are capitalism and socialism; our constitution and preamble draw on both.

Mr. Gordon: When were the British helpful?

Mr. Price: After we started to give them hell, that's in '40s and '50s when we became vocal and began to criticize. We got money from them for clothes, buildings, and education, schools and then agriculture. Yes, they helped. I think the British helped more than the United States, but both of them helped especially in roads and bridges. The United States, though, is too big and too rich to get the feel of everything, but they did help us. The British helped us more when we had self-government, and then other countries came to help us. Israel came to help us.

The Canadian International Development Association has been very helpful. Belize and Canada both belong to The Commonwealth, and I don't like to say this, but [Canada's help came] because of my friendship with Trudeau. He and I were good friends, and he tried to help us. He did his best; in fact, there were some people in Canada criticizing him for too much friendship. I used to go and visit him, and Trudeau would put me up with him, not in his personal home, but in the official house right across the street. He and I were friends, very good friends. He would come to an offshore island and have a chance to do diving. And I would see him in Ottawa.

Socialism and Agriculture

Mr. Gordon: The socialist movement is surely embodied by Assad Shoman who was very attracted to cooperatives with the idea that the *campesinos* (farmers) should work together, that they should share and produce together. What are your impressions of the cooperative movement?

Mr. Price: I supported Assad a lot in his work. Some people call him a communist. I don't think he's a communist. You have to get down to the people and bring them up. We had to get them ready for independence, and we had to educate them in being good citizens, being responsible; and now our aim is not to be a millionaire country, but we get along with the rest of the world [and are trying to] to build our infrastructure.

Mr. Gordon: In building up the country, where did you not have support?

Mr. Price: We had support from the *campesinos* [farmers, largely Maya-Mestizos], they were there from the start. However, those people in the big cities had most things; they were the opposition, so I had to go and talk to them sometimes, give public speeches, and give them a lot of indoctrination.

There is a lot more to do, to put the fire in the politicians to serve the nation. Now they are going into political life to get rich. I have told my colleagues that if you want to get rich, go into business the right way, not go in politics and try to make money. Go into business, making deals. We try to keep the politicians straight. Obviously they don't like my telling them that, [especially] when I tell them we must serve the people. Rather than politicians taking money for some project, we work hard for the poor people making advances in electrical power, hydroelectricity, and agriculture. Let us not forget agriculture—that's the backbone of the country.

Mr. Gordon: But there are some who say that the condition of being a *milpero* and being a subsistence farmer has not improved, and that the Belizean people have not really mechanized efficiently or sought an export market.

Mr. Price: The Mennonites have helped a lot, in the north and the west. Their land reform and cooperatives produced food for themselves and for an export market. They contributed to agricultural progress.

Mr. Gordon: Did you ever reflect on how the Belizean men and women may think when they see these middle Europeans being so successful, how they feel? How does that make a Belizean Maya or Creole feel?

Mr. Price: The Mennonites were protected by the emperors of Russia. Catherine of Russia was their protector, despite Rasputin.

The Mixed Economy

Mr. Gordon: You have seen within the PUP a split; it sort of resembles the Republican-Democratic split in the U.S. How did you handle that? I mean, you have to satisfy the conservative business-minded elements and the socialist elements.

Mr. Price: You have to keep both of them from exceeding their own philosophy; they must share with others, and especially the businessmen must share. I think one of the encyclicals (the Quadragesimo) of Pope Pius XI speaks of sharing the wealth. We are not trying to take everything away [from the rich] but we do want justice in helping others to come up.

Mr. Gordon: As I talk to you, your philosophy sounds so much like Felipe Gonzales, the Prime Minister of Spain (1982–96) and a proponent of a "mixed economy." Was he a friend of yours?

Mr. Price: In a way yes, we used to meet at General Torrijo's home, a very good friend of mine. We used to meet there with [Prime Minister José Maria] Aznar (Prime Minister of Spain 1996–2004). There, we used to meet all those people.

Mr. Gordon: And you were also associated with Fidel Castro?

Mr. Price: Yes, I liked Fidel. He gave me … honored me with some distinction.

Reflections on His Life

Mr. Gordon: How do you think people around you viewed you? Did people around you seek to emulate you?

Mr. Price: I think so. I like having them around; they sort of see how I conduct myself, how I work, the work I do, and then they try to do it,

Mr. Gordon: Who are some of the people you would say sought specifically to be like you?

Mr. Price: Well, I wouldn't say exactly like me, but I would say some members of the People's United Party, such as Assad and Said Musa; other leaders too like Hector Silva (previously, a legislator from Cayo), and there has been long list of members in the People's United Party.

Mr. Price: But I have no troubles talking with Lord Ashcroft [a Belizean billionaire] as well.

Mr. Gordon: You certainly have a gift of communication.

Mr. Price: Well, that's what they say but, but I didn't see it that way. I was just able to communicate with people. I have no formal education; I never went to a university, but I did live among the people.

Notes

Notes to Chapter 1

1. Dengue, a little-recognized disease, has been prevalent in Central America, occasionally in epidemic proportions. To access my consulting work on dengue, see Gordon 1990.

2. Arvigo has produced a considerable amount of literature. Earlier in her career, two books helped establish the area as a center of Maya healing. See Rosita Arvigo 1994, and Rosita Arvigo, Michael Ballick, and Laura Evans 1993. *Rainforest Remedies: 100 Healing Herbs of Belize.* Twin Lakes, WI: Lotus Press.

3. The articulation of these theoretical positions by anthropologists and others is discussed in greater length throughout the book and in the notes here.

4. The presence of African populations and their culture has been an important contribution to scholarship on Central America. A sound scholarly account of African heritage in Belize is provided in Assad Shoman 2010. See also Michael Cutler 1990, "Afro-Caribbean Presence in Central America," *Belizean Studies* 18 no. 2/3: 6–42, and Mathew Restall 2009.

5. Although its Hispanic population continues to grow, the identity of the country has become more solidly Creole. Belize belongs to the economic and political association of Caribbean nations, CARICOM (Caribbean Community), not the Central American alliance of CAFTA (Central American Free Trade Agreement). When one enters Belize taking ground transportation from Mexico or Guatemala, the music on the buses changes from Hispanic tunes and language to what is popular in the Caribbean world and Belize—mostly reggaeton, reggae, Calypso, or the variants of the Caribbean beat in homegrown Belizean Punta Rock and Brukdown. Before 1980, some statistics may be unreliable, for instance the record about the number of Creoles in 1946, as reported by Assad Shoman, should be treated with caution due to the problem of classification and admixture. See page 40 of Assad Shoman 1979.

Notes to Chapter 2

1. Description of Ford's El Pilar project may be accessed through the Website of the Mesoamerican Research Center, headed by Anabel Ford. See http://dev.marc.ucsb .edu, last accessed on April 5, 2012.

2. Many were involved in helping to fashion the future of Belize as a tourist attraction including the United States Agency for International Development (USAID). I refer the reader to the feasibility study by K. Joaquin Glaser-Kohler and Angela Betancourt 1989. In the 1990s, the Blackstone Corporation Resource Management and Tourism consultants in Toronto provided critical assistance thanks to funding from the Inter-American Development Bank. For a brief and refreshing look at the development of tourism I refer the reader to Tom Barry 1995. This book gives an insightful picture of Belize at the time when El Pilar was being developed.

3. The history of the project in great detail was available to me from extensive files in the metal file drawers of the Cultural Center and the consulting firm Help for Progress in Belmopan, Belize. I found out about Kevin Veach's contribution from his report. See Veach Nd. See pages 10–12 for the cited information.

4. The communication about eco-archeology was in a memo to Elias Awe from Anabel Ford, dated December 14, 2001, in the files of Help for Progress.

5. Ample files on the project were also found in the Department of Archeology. The letter from the acting commissioner was dated August 6, 2001, and the letter from the Director of Research was dated December 17, 2003.

6. Estimates of the Maya population of Belize at the height of the Maya Civilization are available in a brief and lucid booklet by Jaime Awe 2005. Reference to population size appears on page 24.

7. I am indebted to the Belizean Tourism Bureau for providing statistical information on the flows and destinations of tourists to Belize.

8. The full name of this institute is the Agroforestry Association, or the *Asociación Coordinadora Indígena y Campesina de Agroforestería Comunitaria Centroamericana*, commonly referred to by its acronym ACICAFOC. It's funding comes from major world organizations such as the World Bank, the United States Agency for International Development, and the European Community.

9. In Chapter 2, the early work of American anthropologist Eric Wolf was an important influence on anthropologists and other social scientists in investigating patron–client relations. Likely Wolf chose to use the word "patron" because it was important in understanding Mexico, the subject of his early research. See Eric Wolf 1966. Other social scientists have explored patron–client relations throughout Latin America. See Strickon, Arnold and Greenfield, Sidney M. eds. 1975. Further examples of the broad geographic range of patron–client relations include James 1972, Sharon Timor 2011, and Andrew Yeos 2006.

Notes to Chapter 3

1. This chapter is strongly influenced by the theoretical framework proposed by Appadurai. See Appadurai 1996, pages 27–47.

2. The subject of "racial relations" between Creoles and Maya-Mestizos is frequently discussed but rarely in such a trenchant way as Laurie Kroshus Medina's article in 2003.

3. Reports on Creole positions appear in Assad Shoman 2010. Peter Ashdown has extensively studied the expressed discontent of Creoles. See page 33 of his 1990 publication for his comments on discharged soldiers.

4. Evan X. Hyde is quite explicit about his early feelings toward George Price. See page 59 of Evan X. Hyde 1995.

5. Those wanting to learn more about Evan X. Hyde's role and influence should go to the source and read his 1995 book, and chapters 7 and 10 of Assad Shoman 2000. Comments about "brilliant historical propaganda" appear on page 140.

6. Extensive literature exists on Marcus Garvey. For a brief biographical sketch I refer the reader to Rupert Lewis 1988. On page 59 the reader will find the mandate of the United Negro Improvement Association.

7. References to Garvey's visit to Belize are contained in Robert A. Hill 1983–85. See especially pages 292–293. For information on Garvey's inauspicious return see page 21 in Ashdown 1990.

8. Shoman reports on the popularization of the African image in Shoman 2000, page 229.

9. A bookshelf of histories and biographies is available on Marley and reggae. One author I would especially recommend is Timothy White, who published a book on Marley in 2006. He brings to the reader the particulars of Marley's life and career, including the meeting between Marley and Wayne Perkins on pages 234–35. See the next page of the text for the nature of this meeting.

10. In documenting the movement of drugs through Central America, I came across evidence of extraordinary freedom of movement of drugs. My search led me to a congressional hearing in which testifiers pointed to the complicity of the U.S. government in international trafficking into the United States. I refer the reader to the hearing before the Committee on Foreign Affairs, House of Representatives, Ninety-Ninth Congress, first session, June 27, 1985. Washington: U.S. G.P.O., 1985. More detailed research on U.S. government complicity appears in several books; see Gary Webb, Gary 1999, and Peter Dale Scott and Jonathan Marshall 1991.

11. Travel guidebooks are a great way to detect the magnets drawing travelers to destinations across the globe. In my research I came across a book that featured Belize and Caye Caulker. See Philippe Gloaguen and Pierre Josse (translated by Mark Howson) 1985. The quote about reggae and dancing is on page 116.

Notes to Chapter 4

1. In writing this chapter, I was very dependent on Assad Shoman (2000). Chapter 9 of this book was fundamental to my understanding of George Price and the formation of the People's United Party and the United Democratic Party. Shoman was personally important in providing information to me through email in March 2012, when he recalled the early days of the cooperative movement and the Solidarity Concerts that led up to the movement itself instead.

2. Although the cooperative movement began in 1979, one earlier experience with cooperatives occurred about the time when George Price started his program of land redistribution. In 1969, the government took 2000 acres of land away from the Samuels' family and turned it over for use as a cooperative by some villagers. This was a short-led and failed experiment.

3. Comments on the importance of cooperatives appear on page 3 of the book by Constance Mungall 1986. The references to grain poultry, feed, and fertilizer may be found in the proposal submitted to Minister Monique Landry, External Relations and International Development by Ian MacPherson, Alex Gracie, and Gerald Schuler of the Canadian Co-operative Association, December 7, 1989.

4. The Canadian Cooperative Association (CCA), was the principal source of support for the cooperative movement in Bullet Tree Falls, and provided the greatest support of any agency to the Canadian cooperative movement throughout the twentieth century and beyond. Its name was the Canadian Union of Operatives until 1987, when it changed to the Canadian Co-Operative Association.

5. I found a description of the depressed conditions of Nova Scotia in the article, entitled "The World Comes to Antigonish," *Weekend Magazine*, October 1, 1966.

6. Alexander Laidlaw affiliated with the University of St. Francis Xavier and the CCA edited the writings of Coady in Alexander F. Laidlaw, 1971, *The Man from Margaree: Writings and Speeches of M.M. Coady*, edited and with a commentary by Alexander F. Laidlaw, Toronto: McClelland and Steward, Limited. Coady's citation from Pope Pius XI's Quadragesimo and his commentaries about his priorities in education and cooperatives come from pages 119–120, and his citation of Pope Pius XI comes from page 128 of the same work.

7. The Canadian Co-operative Association, like any recipient of a significant amount of federal money, was always called on to defend and define itself. The comments here about a favorable environment are from its *Programme Presentation 1988/89 to 1990/91*.

8. I refer the reader to an insightful book about parallel political changes in Canada, the United States, and England, written by Donald Savior 1994.

9. In 1985, new efforts arose to enhance the San Miguel and Bullet Tree Livestock cooperatives. Also in this year, the cooperative movement expanded to include the Western Livestock Cooperative in 1986, and a second retail cooperative in 1987. The conduct and fate of the aforementioned cooperatives repeat patterns of the earlier cooperatives—mistrust of leaders, lack of cooperation, individualism, accusations of theft if not theft itself, and the inability of NGOs to intervene. The Western Livestock was located a mile from the El Pilar Site. The other cooperative retail outlet was on the western or Guatemalan side of town. The importance of "apex organization" is explained on page 11, volume 1 of a 1988 evaluation of a CCA activities conducted by the consulting firm Horizon Pacific in Duncan, British Columbia. Also see Ian MacPherson (nd). On page 19 he makes reference to the importance of the "apex strategy" for the delivering of services.

10. Comments about the inability of the CCA to meet the needs of cooperatives are in the planning report entitled *Co-Operative Union of Canada. International Development Program 1987/88* Ottawa, Canada: Canadian Co-Operative Union found in Library and Archives of Canada, on page 4.

Notes to Chapter 5

1. In this chapter I have accounted for all Social Gospel Evangelical churches and Pentecostal churches. Several years before my research, a new church was formed by the Baptists, called the "Baptist Bullet Tree Church." Because the church serves recent Central American settlers residing in the hills outside the village, I did not consider it to be part of the fabric of the village life. I knew of no people residing in the village center or the immediate periphery who were members of this church.

2. For a concise and straightforward description of the origin and function of Catholic rituals, see Ann Ball 2003. The discussion on page 502 of her book deals with the displacement of indigenous worship.

3. Many anthropologists have written insightfully about the smooth displacement of indigenous beliefs by the Catholic faith, especially Nancy Farriss 1994 and James Watanabe 1990.

4. The connectedness of altered states of consciousness and religion has been a central concern in the subfield of the anthropology of religion. I refer readers

interested in shamanism to the "dean" of studies on shamans, Mircea Eliade (1972). Lest we think that these practices are solely the province of "primitive peoples," Felicitas Goodman who spent a lifetime studying Mexican Maya has set us straight. She described how twentieth-century Maya Pentecostal leaders closely resemble shamans. See Goodman, Felicitas 1971. Information on the biological substrate of shamanism appears in Michael Winkelman's Chapter 10 called "The Shamanic Paradigm of Ethnomedicine" in his book *Culture in Health: Applying Medical Anthropology*, San Francisco: Jossey Bass, 2009. For a quick and entertaining take on the biological substrate of worship see the YouTube presentation by Michael Harner in his "Transcendence of Time," www.youtube.com/watch?v=27DCN0f_1fc. Last accessed October 14, 2012.

5. The origins of the connection between Azusa Street as well as the growth of the Pentecostal Church is traced by one fervent believer in the Pentecostal Church of God, Aaron M. Wilson 2001.

6. Aside from Harvey Cox's wise comment, readers may gain a deeper appreciation of the importance of the Azusa Street Movement in American religion through reading Joseph Creech Jr. 1996. The outreach of the church is discussed in Grant A. Wacker 1999.

7. Appreciating the two poles of religious life, intense spirituality versus civic commitment is central to an understanding of American religion and the growth of Protestant America. The importance of the spiritual side of the growing religious tenor of America is made clear in Donald G. Mathews 1969. In the Ronald Numbers book, especially consult pages 189–199.

8. For insight into the impressive numerical growth of the Adventist church domestically and abroad, see George R. Knights (1999), especially pages 132–146, containing information on the growth of the church.

9. I heard much of the story of the Mundall family from Dr. Raymond Mundall's son, Dr. John Mundall, who asked me to remind readers that the growth of the Adventists under his father's watch had been "a testimony to the Glory of God."

10. The Loma Luz Website is: Loma+Luz+Hospital%2C+Belize&rlz=1C1FLDB_enAR568AR568&oq=Loma+Luz+Hospital%2C+Belize&aqs=chrome.69i57.10937j0j4&sourceid=chrome&es_sm=122&ie=UTF-8. Last accessed April 5, 2012.

11. Cognitive anthropology is a subfield that gives narratives close attention in explaining behavior. For a more comprehensive understanding of D'Andrade's contributions to cognitive anthropology, I refer the reader to Roy D'Andrade 1995; also to Naomi Quinn and Dorothy Holland, eds. 1987, *Cultural Models in Language and Thought* New York: Cambridge University Press, and my own work in West Africa: Andrew J. Gordon 2000.

Notes to Chapter 6

1. For further explanation of the advantages of using a transtheoretical approach, the reader should see James O. Prochaska 2014.

Bibliography

Anderson, Allen. 2004. *An Introduction to Pentecostalism*. Cambridge: Cambridge University Press.

Anderson, Benedict. 1983. *Imagined Communities: Reflections on the Origin and Spread of Nationalism*. New York: Verso Press.

Appadurai, Arjun. 1996. *From Modernity at Large: Cultural Dimensions of Globalization*. Minneapolis, MN: University of Minnesota Press.

Arvigo, Rosita. 1994. *Sastun: My Apprenticeship with a Maya Healer*. San Francisco: Harper.

Arvigo, Rosita, Michael Ballick, and Laura Evans. 1993. *Rainforest Remedies: 100 Healing Herbs of Belize*. Twin Lakes, WI: Lotus Press.

Ashdown, Peter. 1990. Garveyism in Belize. *SPEAReports 5*. Benque Viejo, Belize: Cubola Productions.

Awe, Jaime. 2005. *Ancient Maya of Belize*. Belize City: Factory Books.

Ball, Ann. 2003. *Encyclopedia of Catholic Devotions and Practices*. Houston: Our Sunday Visitor Publishing Division.

Barry, Tom with Dylan Vernon. 1995. *Inside Belize* 2nd Ed. Albuquerque, NM: The Interhemispheric Resource Center.

Belliveau, Jeannette. 2006. *Romance on the Road: Travelling Women Who Love Foreign Men*. Baltimore, MD: Beau Monde Press.

Brown, David F. and Jeanne M. Wolfe. 1997. Adjusting Planning Frameworks to Meet Changing Needs in Countries: The Example of Belize. *Habitat International* 21(1): 51–63.

Cox, Harvey. 1996. *Fire from Heaven: The Rise of Pentecostal Spirituality and the Reshaping of Religions in the Twenty-First Century*. London: Cassell.

Creech Jr., Joseph W. 1996. Vision of Glory: The Place of Azusa Street in Pentecostal History. *Church History* 65(3): 405–424.

Damsteegt, P. Gerard. 1977. *Foundations of the Seventh-Day Adventist Message and Mission*. Grand Rapids MI: Eerdmans Publishing Company.

D'Andrade, Roy. 1995. *The Development of Cognitive Anthropology*. New York: Cambridge University Press.

Downing, Theodore E. 1996. Mitigating Impoverishment When People are Involuntarily Displaced. In *Understanding Impoverishment: The Consequences of Development and Induced Displacement*, ed Christopher McDowell, 33–48. Oxford, U.K.: Berghahn Books.

Eliade, Mircea. 1972. *Shamanism: Archaic Techniques of Ecstasy*. Princeton, NJ: Princeton University Press.

Farriss, Nancy. 1984. *Maya Society under Colonial Rule: The Collective Enterprise of Survival*. Princeton: Princeton University Press.

Finke, Roger and Rodney Stark. 1989. How the Upstart Sects Won America: 1776–1850. *Journal for the Scientific Study of Religion* 28(1): 26–44.

Glaser-Kohler K Joaquin and Angela Betancourt. 1989. *Feasibility Study of Archeological Development to Stimulate Tourism: Site Identification, Infrastructure Needs and Investment Requirements*. Presented to USAID/Belize and the government of Belize. Belmopan, Belize: Help for Progress.

Gloaguen, Philippe and Pierre Josse (translated by Mark Howson). 1985. *Mexico, Belize, and Guatemala and the French Antilles*. New York: Macmillan Publishing Company, Collier World Traveler Series.

Goodman, Felicitas. 1972. *Speaking in Tongues: A Cross-Cultural Study of Glossolalia*. Chicago: University of Chicago Press.

Gordon, Andrew. 2000. Cultural Identity and Illness: Fulani Views. *Culture, Medicine, and Psychiatry* 24(3): 297–330.

Gordon, Andrew. 1990. *Community Participation and Vector-Borne Disease Control in Belize: An Assessment of*

Current and Potential Activities.
Washington, DC: Office of Health,
Bureau of Science and Technology,
U.S. Agency for International
Development.

Haley, Alex. 1976. *Roots*. Garden City, NY:
Doubleday.

Harner, Michael. *The Transcendence of
Time in Shamanic Practice.* www
.youtube.com/watch?v=27DCN0f_1fc,
last accessed October 14, 2012.

Hinkle, B.L. 2010. *Just a Passin' Thru':
The Story of the Ernest Parnell Family
and Their Pioneering Traveling Ministry.* Guthrie, OK: Daisy Mae Publishing
LLC.

Hill, Robert A. 1983–85. *Marcus Garvey
and UNIA Papers Vol. III.* Los Angeles:
UCLA Press.

Hyde, Evan X. 1995. *X Communication:
Selected Writings.* Belize City: The
Angelus Press Ltd.

Knight, George R. 1999. *Walking with Ellen
White: The Human Interest Story.*
Hagerstown, MD: Review and Herald
Publications Association.

Laidlaw, Alexander F., ed. 1971. *The Man
from Margaree: Writings and Speeches
of M.M. Coady,* edited and with a
commentary by Alexander F. Laidlaw.
Toronto: McClelland and Steward,
Limited.

Lewis, Rupert. 1988. *Marcus Garvey: Anti-
Colonial Champion.* Trenton, NJ:
Africa World Press, Inc.

Lisbey, Joe. 2008. *Reorganization and
Strengthening of the Department of
Co-operative.* TCP/BZE/3101 9D –
Belize FAO Project, Cayo, Belize.

Lotz, Jim. 2005. *The Humble Giant: Moses
Coady, Canada's Rural Revolutionary.*
Ottawa, Canada: Novalis, St. Paul
University.

MacPherson, Ian. nd. *The History of the
Canadian Co-operative Movement: A
Summary, a Little Historiography, and
Some Issues.*

MacAndrew, Craig and Robert B. Edgerton.
1969. *Drunken Comportment: A Social
Explanation.* Chicago: Aldine.

Mathews, Donald G. 1969. The
Second Great Awakening as an
Organizing Process, 1780–1830: A
hypothesis. *American Quarterly* 21(1):
23–43.

McPherson, Anne. 1995. Introduction. In
Backtalking Belize: Selected Writings,
Assad Shoman, I–XV. Belize: Angelus
Press Limited.

McPherson, Grant. nd. *Between Here and
There.* Santa Elena, Belize: Loma Linda
Hospital.

Medina Lauri Kroshus. 2003. History, Culture, and Place-Making: 'Native' status
and Maya Identity in Belize. In *Perspectives on Las Américas,* eds. Matthew C. Gutmann et al., 195–212.
Malden, MA: Blackwell Publishing
Company.

Morgan, Douglas. 2001. *Adventism and the
American Republic: The Public
Involvement of a Major Apocalyptic
Movement.* Knoxville: The University
of Tennessee Press.

Mungall, Constance. 1986. *More Than Just
a Job: Worker Cooperatives in Canada.*
Ottawa: Steel Rail.

Numbers, Ronald. 1976. *Prophetess of
Health: Ellen G. White.* New York:
Harper & Row, Publishers.

People's United Party. 1979. *Manifesto for
the New and Progressive Revolution.*
Belize City, Belize: People's United
Party.

Pilcha, Janet B. 2011. Mentoring. *Federally
Employed Women's News* 43(2): 1.

Primer, Ben. 1979. *Protestants and American Business Methods.* Ann Arbor, MI:
UMI Research Press.

Prochaska, James O. 2014. *Systems of Psy-
chotherapy: A Transtheoretical Analysis.* Stamford, CT: Cengage Learning.

Quinn, Naomi and Dorothy Holland, eds.
1987. *Cultural Models in Language and
Thought.* New York: Cambridge University Press.

Restall, Mathew. 2009. *The Black Middle:
Africans, Mayas, and Spaniards in
Colonial Yucatan.* Stanford, CA:
Stanford University Press.

San Miguel. 1983. *1er Laboratorio Experi-
mental Yo Sayab Para la Formación de
Cuadros Organizadores de Cooperati-
vas. Cooperativa San Miguel.* Cayo,
Belice. 6 al 26 de Marzo. Bullet Tree
Falls, Cayo. Belize.

Savior, Donald J. 1994. *Thatcher, Reagan,
Mulroney: In Search of a New
Bureaucracy.* Pittsburgh, PA: Univer-
sity of Pittsburgh Press.

Scott, James. 1972. The Erosion of Patron-Client Bonds and Social Change in Rural Southeast Asia. *Journal of Asian Studies* 32(1): 5–37.

Scott, Peter Dale and Jonathan Marshall. 1991. *Cocaine Politics: Drugs, Armies, and the CIA in Central America*, updated edition. Berkeley and Los Angeles: University of California.

Shoman, Assad. 2010. Reflections on Ethnicity and Nation. *Belize Cuaderno de Trabajo 9* AFRODESC: 2–61.

_____. 2000. *Thirteen Chapters of a History of Belize*. Belize City: Angelus Press.

_____. 1979. Birth of the Nationalist Movement in Belize. BISRA Occasional Publication # 7. Belize City, Belize.

_____. 1995. *Backtalking Belize: Selected Writings*, ed. Anne S MacPherson. Belize City, Belize: Angelus Press Limited.

Stone, Michael Cutler. 1990. Afro-Caribbean Presence in Central America, *Belizean Studies* 18(no. 2/3): 6–42.

Strickon, Arnold and Sidney M. Greenfield eds. 1975. *Structure and Process in Latin America*. Albuquerque, NM: The University of New Mexico.

Sutherland, Anne. 1998. *The Making of Belize: Globalization in the Margins*. Westport, CT: Bergin & Garvey.

Timor, Sharon. 2011. The Dynamics of Elite Networks and Patron–Client Relations in Afghanistan. *Europe-Asia Studies* 63(6): 1109–1127.

Turner, Frederick Jackson. 1994. The Significance of the Section (1925), 201–224, and The West and American Ideals, (1914), 140–158. In *Rereading Fredrick Jackson Turner*. New York: Henry Holt and Company.

Veach, Kevin. nd. *Final Report for the El Pilar/UF Community Participation Project October, 1997–1998 July*. Bullet Tree Falls: Be Puk Te.

Wacker, Grant A. 1999. Travail of a Broken Family: Radical Evangelical Responses to the Emergence of Pentecostalism in America, 1906–16. In *Pentecostal Currents in American Protestantism*, ed. Edith L. Blumhofer, Russell Spittler and Grant A. Wacker. 23–49. Urbana, IL: University of Illinois Press.

Watanabe, James. 1990. From Saints to Shibboleths: Image, Structure and Identity in Mayan Religious Syncretism. *American Ethnologist* 17(1): 131–150.

Webb, Gary. 1999. *Dark Alliance: The CIA, the Contras, and the Crack Cocaine Explosion*. New York: Seven Stories Press.

White, Ellen G. 2002. *The Great Controversy Ended: A Glimpse into Eternity*. Silver Spring, MD: Better Living Publications.

_____. 1990. *The Colporteur Ministry*. Nampa, ID: Pacific Press Publishing Association.

_____. 1867. *Testimony for the Church No. 11*. Battle Creek, MI: Steam Press of the Seventh-day Adventist Publishing Association.

White, Timothy. 2006. *Catch a Fire: The Life of Bob Marley*. New York: Henry Holt and Company.

Wilson, Aaron M. 2001. *Our Story: The History of the Pentecostal Church of God*. Joplin Missouri: Messenger Publishing House.

Winkelman, Michael. 2009. *Culture in Health: Applying Medical Anthropology*. San Francisco: Jossey Bass.

Wolf, Eric. 1966. Kinship, Friendship and Patron–Client relations. In *The Social Anthropology of Complex Societies, Association of Social Anthropology Monograph #4*. Michael Banton, ed. 71–100. London: Tavistock Press.

Yeos, Andrew. 2006. Signaling Democracy: Patron-Client Relations and Democratization in South Korea and Poland. *Journal of East Asian Studies* 6(2): 259–287.

Index

Page numbers followed by f indicate figure